an illustrated introduction to
THE REGENCY

Mike Rendell and Philippa Sutcliffe

AMBERLEY

The Royal Pavilion, Brighton. (Courtesy of flamenc under Creative Commons 3.0)

First published 2015

Amberley Publishing
The Hill, Stroud
Gloucestershire, GL5 4EP

www.amberley-books.com

British Library Cataloguing in Publication Data.
A catalogue record for this book is available from the British Library.

ISBN 978 1 4456 4682 4 (paperback)
ISBN 978 1 4456 4683 1 (ebook)

Typesetting and Origination by Amberley Publishing.
Printed in Great Britain.

CONTENTS

A SKETCH for a VICEROY!!

Thoughts on a Restricted Regency

A

THE ROYAL JERSEY!

London Published by S.W. Fores 50, Piccadilly. February 22. 1797. NB Folios of Carecatures Lent out for the Evening

THE REGENCY
IN FIVE MINUTES

In its formal sense, the Regency period lasted only nine years. It started on 5 April 1811 when the Regency Act came into force, and lasted until 29 January 1820 when George III died. However, that formal analysis tells only half the story. The Regency era was also a sense of style and fashion, an important turning point in the fortunes of the British nation and a watershed in art and literature. Some may see the Regency as the jam in the sandwich – a period of excitement, colour and vibrant excess set between the rather dour, austere court of George III and the buttoned-up Victorian era. In its wider sense, the Regency can be said to have lasted from 1800 until the death of George IV in 1830, a thirty year period which saw massive changes throughout society. That is the period on which this book concentrates – with the Industrial Revolution spinning faster and faster; a time when with France, which had lasted for over two decades, came to an end with spectacular victories such as those at Trafalgar and Waterloo. It was an era dominated by the personality of the Regent himself, a man renowned for his licentiousness and excess. He very publicly drank, gambled, and womanised in a way which brought shame to the royal family. He alienated his father, and as the Regency progressed he also alienated a large section of the British public with his extravagance. At a time when the nation was being asked to tighten its belt, with food shortages and rampant inflation, people were not endeared towards a ruler who considered it appropriate to demolish his princely palace at Carlton House, barely before

Opposite: 'A sketch for the *Vice*-Roy, The Royal Jarsey' by Isaac Cruikshank, 1797. (Lewis Walpole Library)

the builders had finished it. He spent hundreds of thousands of pounds on modernising and extending Buckingham Palace, which was a home he never lived in. It represented a white elephant and did not become a royal residence until Queen Victoria came to the throne.

On the plus side, the Prince Regent was like a breath of fresh air, a change from the stultifying, cheese-paring atmosphere of the household of George III. Here was a man who was charismatic, full of life, and willing to try new ideas. He encouraged new British artists, many of whom had graduated from the Royal Academy, so that people like Lawrence, Constable and Turner became the generation which succeeded to the mantle of Reynolds and Gainsborough. The prince employed architects such as Henry Holland and John Nash to change the face of the royal residences, developing the neo-classical style borrowed from the French, but then moved on to the extraordinary design hotchpotch which was to become the Royal Pavilion at Brighton. His whimsicality, his willingness to 'break the rules' and to encourage new ideas was highly influential, and it was his taste which helped bring in an upsurge in Graeco-Roman style. The royal residences were filled with elaborate furniture, often using the very best French cabinet-makers, and frequently decorated with much gold-work. Sèvres porcelain was a particular favourite of the prince and he built up a collection of Dutch and Flemish Masterpieces which now form the centrepiece of today's magnificent Royal Collection. He was probably the best art patron of any of the monarchs to ascend the British throne, but on the other hand he took very little notice of the ordinary people he was supposed to serve. He alienated public opinion with his appalling treatment of Caroline, his wife. He loathed her and, not content with being a serial adulterer himself, tried to accuse her of adulterous conduct. Their union had resulted in a legitimate heir (Princess Charlotte) but tragically Charlotte died giving birth to a stillborn baby when she was twenty-one. The prince wanted to divorce Caroline and, when he finally became king in 1820, he banished his wife from attending the coronation. She died in unexplained circumstances just three weeks later.

The 1801 census revealed a population of 9.3 million. The Prince Regent would have associated with perhaps one-tenth of 1 per cent of this figure – maybe 10,000 – those of consequence and position. For this upper echelon, life would consist of idleness or following the pursuits of the elite, being 'part of Society' and its pleasures, especially during the Season. This lifestyle trickled down through lower levels of 'The Quality' depending upon their ability to support it, and was certainly what the new middle classes aspired to. But, for the working classes, life was still very hard indeed. The Regency saw prolonged periods of social unrest, and fears about unemployment lead to the Luddites destroying factory machinery and even to soldiers opening fire on unarmed civilians at Peterloo.

The Regency also saw Jane Austen publish four novels (albeit anonymously) with two posthumous publications helping to cement her reputation as a wonderful observer of manners and etiquette. Mary Shelley's *Frankenstein* came up with a totally different genre of science fiction combined with the horror story. In 1812 the Elgin marbles arrived in London, triggering an interest in the art of Ancient Greece and, in the same year, the waltz first hit the dance floor and outraged traditionalists. 1812 also saw the assassination of the Prime Minister Spencer Perceval.

In 1814 the Prince Regent hosted two significant events when the Allied sovereigns paid a state visit. Tsar Alexander of Russia and King Frederick William III of Prussia came to London to celebrate the (illusory) peace after Napoleon's exile to Elba. It also marked the centenary of the House of Hanover; the Prince Regent's great-great-grandfather George I having acceded to the English throne in 1714. Between June and August there were huge festivities including a formal procession to the Guildhall, balloon ascents, triumphal follies and fireworks in Hyde Park, St James's Park and Green Park. There was also a mock naval battle on the Serpentine. The visiting royalty found time for trips to the Theatre Royal, Ascot races, and to a review of the Fleet at Portsmouth.

In industrial developments the first street lighting appeared, in Pall Mall. An engine called 'Puffing Billy' first ran on rails, and engines designed by Trevethick and Stephenson heralded the dawn of the Railway Age. Davy came up with his safety lamp for workers in ever-deeper mine shafts and a steam-powered vessel crossed the Atlantic for the first time. Engineers Marc Brunel and Henry Maudslay joined forces to come up with machinery capable of driving the Rotherhithe Tunnel under the River Thames and a new bridge spanned the river in place of the increasingly decrepit London Bridge. Around the country new bridges, canals, harbours and breakwaters changed the face of the country, along with great docks being constructed in London's port.

The abolition of the slave trade in the British colonies finally became a reality in 1807, although it would be another twenty-six years before slavery itself would be abolished.

Above all, the Regency period saw etiquette, good manners and style elevated to an art-form. Aided by the likes of Beau Brummell, clothing and appearance became pivotal. Concepts such as honour, refinement, propriety and 'polite society' achieved vital importance, while the 'Beau Monde' and 'the ton' dominated the minds of anyone with pretensions to respectability.

Statue of George IV outside the Royal Pavilion at Brighton. (Author's collection)

TIMELINE

● **1801**
Act of Union unites the parliaments of Great Britain and Ireland.

● **1802**
Peace of Amiens signed by England, France and Spain

● **1803**
War breaks out again, bringing fears of a French invasion.

● **1804**
William Pitt appointed Prime Minister again. Napoleon proclaimed Emperor.

● **1805**
Death of Horatio Nelson at the Battle of Trafalgar.

● **1806**
Deaths of politicians William Pitt (the Younger) and Charles James Fox.

● **1807**
Abolition of colonial slave trading. Gas lighting installed in Pall Mall.

● **1808**
Richard Trevethick runs an early steam engine around a track at Euston.

● **1809**
Death of Matthew Boulton.

● **1810**
George III pronounced insane.

● **1811**
George, Prince of Wales, officially becomes Regent (5 February) and subsequently appoints himself Field Marshal. The Luddites damage factory machinery in the Midlands. Jane Austen's *Sense and Sensibility* is published.

● **1812**
Assassination of Prime Minister Spencer Perceval. America declares war on Britain. Napoleon begins the retreat from Moscow. The waltz is first danced in London ballrooms. Byron publishes first two cantos of 'Childe Harold's Pilgrimage'.

● **1813**
Pride and Prejudice published.

1814

The Thames freezes over in February and the last great Frost Fair is held. Napoleon abdicates and is exiled to Elba. Allied leaders celebrate victory in London with processions and festivals. Congress of Vienna begins. Treaty of Ghent brings peace between England and America.

1815

Napoleon escapes from Elba, raises an army and is defeated at Waterloo (18 June). The Corn Law is passed and leads to riots in London. John Nash starts renovation work at Brighton Pavilion.

1816

Princess Charlotte marries Prince Leopold of Belgium. Beau Brummell flees to France to escape his creditors. The British Museum acquires the Elgin Marbles. It is 'the year without summer'.

1817

Jane Austen dies. Death of Princess Charlotte in childbirth. A spectacular feast is prepared by Antonin Carême for the Prince Regent at Brighton's Royal Pavilion.

1818

Hasty marriages of three of the brothers of the Prince Regent, occasioned by the need to secure a successor.

1819

Birth of Princess Victoria. Peterloo Massacre. Death of James Watt. First steam-propelled vessel (the SS *Savannah*) crosses the Atlantic.

1820

Death of George III (29 January). The Prince Regent is proclaimed George IV. Cato Street conspirators plan to murder the Cabinet. The trial of the king's wife for adultery begins and the Bill of Pains and Penalties is brought before Parliament.

1821

Napoleon dies. George IV's coronation is held in Westminster Abbey (19 July). Deaths of Queen Caroline and John Keats. John Constable exhibits 'The Hay Wain'.

1822

Charles Babbage designs the 'difference engine', an early computing machine. George IV visits Scotland. The Caledonian Canal, engineered by Thomas Telford, links the east and west coasts of Scotland.

1823

The Lancet is first printed. Death of Edward Jenner, smallpox pioneer.

1824

First pile driven for the new London Bridge. Formation of the Society for Prevention of Cruelty to Animals. The Vagrancy Act makes begging a criminal offence.

1825

Work begins on the Thames Tunnel. The first horse-drawn omnibus appears on London's streets.

1826

Formation of London Zoological Society. Menai Suspension Bridge links Anglesey with the Welsh mainland.

1827

Death of artist and poet William Blake. Marble Arch erected at Buckingham Palace.

1828

Trial of body snatchers Burke and Hare. Death of rocket pioneer William Congreve.

1829

Foundation of Metropolitan Police Service by Robert Peel, with headquarters at Scotland Yard. Catholic Relief Act brings Catholic emancipation. Stephenson's Rocket wins the Rainhill Trials

1830

Death of George IV and accession of William IV. Swing Riots in Kent spread across the south east of England. Edwin Budding invents the lawnmower.

George, Prince of Wales, by Sir William Beechey. (Metropolitan Museum of Art. Accession Number: 1986.264.3)

1
FROM PRINCE OF WALES
TO PRINCE REGENT

George Augustus Frederick, Prince of Wales, was born in 1762, two years after his father, George III, had come to the throne. In his mid-twenties he started to get frustrated at kicking his heels waiting to take over from a father seen as being distant, boring and old-fashioned. Young George had already sampled the delights of high-living, with his father convinced that it was the dissolute rake Charles James Fox who had led him astray. It is fair to say that young George did not need much persuading, becoming a regular drinking, gambling and whoring companion to not just Fox, but the playwright Richard Brinsley Sheridan, the Barrymore brothers, and the likes of Colonel Hanger, the fourth Baron Coleraine. Together with a swathe of hangers-on, the prince and his set saw themselves as untouchable; they drank as if their livers would last forever; they gambled tens of thousands of pounds at a single session as if the money pot would never run dry; they kept company with whores regardless of the consequences.

One of his early conquests was an impecunious (but married) actress called Mary Robinson. He saw her performing the role of Perdita in *A Winter's Tale* at the Drury Lane Theatre when he was just seventeen. He was besotted with her, and instructed Lord Malden to open negotiations with a view to her becoming his mistress. Terms were eventually agreed – she would be paid a 'signing on fee' of £20,000, payable at age twenty-one, and this was backed up by a legally binding bond. She succumbed to this lucrative offer, was showered with gifts, and quickly became a famous celebrity, with her own carriage and liveried footmen. She was, however, permanently living beyond her means, and when the tight-fisted prince grew bored and wanted to move on from Perdita, he tried to go back on the deal. Eventually he settled for paying her a much lesser sum, in return for her handing back some of his more indiscreet love letters.

In 1785 the prince went through a form of marriage with the twice-widowed Maria Fitzherbert. It could never be valid, since the consent of the king and the Privy Council had not been sought and the ceremony contravened the Royal

'The Goats canter to Windsor, or the Cuckold's Comfort.' Published in 1784, this shows the Prince of Wales, accompanied by Mary Robinson, driving his high gig drawn by six goats. Charles Fox acts as lead rider while in the foreground Mr Robinson, the cuckolded husband, is shown riding a goat back to front. (Lewis Walpole Library)

Marriages Act. Maria was a Roman Catholic and, if the necessary consent had been obtained, it would automatically have barred the prince from ever becoming king due to the provisions of the Bill of Rights and the Act of Settlement of 1701. The wedding was therefore a secret affair, officiated over by a clergyman imprisoned as a debtor in the Fleet Prison. His debts were cleared by the prince in return for his co-operation and silence. Rumours subsequently surfaced of one or more children born to Maria, and presumably fathered by the Prince of Wales, but there is no conclusive proof of this.

Three years later Prince George was entertaining thoughts of taking over from his father, when the king's frequent bouts of illness led many to question whether a regency was needed. There were fears that the king's mental state could mean that he was unfit to deliver the King's Speech at the opening session of Parliament. There was a debate as to whether the Prince of Wales should automatically be sole regent, or whether Parliament could make some other selection. In the event, the Regency Bill was passed in 1788 but then hit the buffers because, without the

Royal Assent, it could never become law. At that point the king recovered and the bill was shelved, but later, in 1811, it would be dusted off and reused. This time, King George would give his assent.

Back in 1788 the disappointed prince carried on spending extravagantly. Having moved on from Mary Robinson, he conducted a number of lesser affairs with courtesans and common whores. His conquests also included the divorcée Grace Elliott, later 'passed on' to the Duc d'Orleans, and the Countess of Jersey with whom he had a lengthy affair starting in 1793. By then, she was a forty-year-old grandmother, a mother of ten children, and very much married to George Villiers, who was promptly recompensed for being cuckolded by being made Master of the Horse to the Prince of Wales. The Countess of Jersey was the prince's unchallenged 'senior mistress', running his household for over ten years until she was supplanted by the Marchioness of Hertford in 1807. Some thirty years earlier, as a sixteen-year old, she had married the Marquis of Hertford and, although her husband tried to end the royal affair by sending his wife to Ireland, she became the prince's mistress and continued as such until 1817. The prince then turned his attentions towards the matronly Marchioness Conyngham. She too was married, but presumably her husband considered it a great honour to be cuckolded by someone so eminent …

The prince's finances were a disaster. By 1795 he owed a staggering £630,000. The king would only agree to offer financial assistance if the prince agreed to 'settle down and get married' to his cousin Princess Caroline of Brunswick. The couple had never even met, and the prince could not stand the look of his bride, claiming that she needed a good bath. The marriage in April 1795 was a disaster and the couple split permanently once Caroline had given birth to a daughter Charlotte, the only legitimate issue the prince ever had. In 1804, custody of Charlotte was taken away from her mother, who stood accused by her husband of having had another child by an unnamed lover. A Parliamentary Commission was called to look into the allegation which, although unproved, did show that Caroline had behaved very indiscreetly. The marriage breakdown polarised popular opinion, with Jane Austen famously writing to her friend Martha Lloyd in 1813: 'I will always support her as long as I can, because she is a woman, and because I hate her husband… I am resolved at least always to think that she would have been respectable, if the Prince had behaved only tolerably by her at first.'

For the next twenty years George tried to get a divorce, but was persuaded that in a court of law his own infidelities would become the focus of attention

Portrait of a lady, thought to be Maria Fitzherbert, by John Hoppner. (Metropolitan Museum of Art. Gift of William T. and Eleanor Blodgett. Accession Number: 06.1242)

Above left: 'Queen Caroline. Britain's best hope!! England's sheet-anchor!!' by John Fairburn. This dates from 1820. (Courtesy of the Library of Congress)

Above right: The Prince Regent in 1816 by Henry Bone (painted on enamel, after Sir Thomas Lawrence). (Metropolitan Museum of Art; Bequest of Collis P. Huntington, 1900. Accession Number: 26.168.61)

and cause great embarrassment to the monarchy. Matters eased when Caroline moved abroad in 1814 – at least her indiscretions were less obvious to the Regent, although stories that she was openly living with her Italian lover Bartolomeo Pergami soon filtered back to England, causing the caricaturists to go into overdrive with pictures of the unlikely couple (she was squat and unprepossessing; he, vastly taller and bearded).

One thing was already certain when the king came to the throne in 1820: at fifty-eight years old, he was unlikely to produce a legitimate heir, following the death of his twenty-one-year-old daughter Charlotte in 1817. Poor Charlotte – she had spent her childhood torn between her conflicting parents, ending up in an isolated existence imposed by her father, unable to choose her own friends and expected to stay out of the public gaze. She was, however, something of a wild child, keen to kick over the traces, and reportedly had a number of unsuitable alliances with impecunious young men. The Regent decided that his daughter should be married off, preferably to William, Prince of Orange, but Charlotte was totally unimpressed when she met the prince, and guessed what her father was up to. She felt compelled to sign a contract agreeing to the marriage, but subsequently imposed conditions which made it absolutely certain that the prince would not accept, for instance that Charlotte's mother should live with them both, or that she should never be expected to leave England. The engagement was swiftly broken off. By then, Charlotte had fallen for the charms of a young Lieutenant-General in the Russian cavalry by the name of Prince Leopold of Saxe-Coburg-Saalfeld. He had no money, but in time Charlotte managed to talk her father round to approving the match. They got engaged to great public acclaim in March 1816; Parliament voted Prince Leopold a sum of £50,000 and bought the couple a home known as Claremont House. The wedding in May that year was a spectacular affair, held at Carlton House, and the wedding dress alone was reputed to have cost £10,000. They were a golden couple, adored by the public which saw them as a breath of fresh air after the increasingly unattractive, obese and unlovely Prince Regent. Charlotte quickly became pregnant, but miscarried. She got pregnant again, and carried the baby for the full term before being delivered of a stillborn child on 5 November 1817. She had endured a terrible labour lasting over three days, and amid accusations of negligence on the part of her physician Sir Richard Croft, she developed puerperal fever and died the following day. Her father, her husband, and the whole nation were distraught and went into a lengthy period of mourning. The Regent was too unwell even to attend the funeral. Meanwhile no-one thought to inform Caroline, Princess of Wales that both her child and grandchild had died, and she only heard out about it from a passing messenger.

Charlotte's death, and the increasingly obvious fact that the Prince Regent was never likely to father another heir, meant great pressure was brought to bear on the various philandering younger brothers of the Regent. William, the next in line, had been living with his mistress Dorothea Jordan for twenty years and had sired at least ten illegitimate children by her. He unhitched himself from the long-suffering Dorothea and scoured Europe for a suitable princess to marry – not easy, given that he was fifty-three and had a somewhat colourful past, to say nothing of the nine children who were still living with him. Eventually the twenty-five year old Princess Adelaide of Saxe-Meiningen accepted his marriage proposal and they were wed in 1818. It became a bit of a race to see which of the royal brothers could come up with a child first, and cartoonists had a field day. The Regent's younger brother Prince Edward, Duke of Kent had taken the hint. He had been living in Brussels with his mistress, Julie de St Laurent. He ditched her and married Prince Leopold's sister, Victoria. They went on to have a child called Princess Alexandrina Victoria of Kent. In 1837 she would accede to the throne as Queen Victoria, but all that was very much in the future.

Where to live was his first concern. His existing home at Carlton House was largely remodelled before the Regency period. It was the house which had come to him via his grandmother and Parliament had awarded him the sum of £60,000 to cover refurbishments. Hundreds of thousands of pounds later, it was still not finished to his satisfaction. It was lavishly furnished and extended over and over again until it was the most opulent of princely palaces. But when George became king he felt that it really was not sufficiently regal, so he decided to pull the entire edifice down to the ground. He employed John Nash to remodel what was the Queen's House and to transform it into a palace fit for a king. It became known as Buckingham Palace. The old building had been adequate for Queen

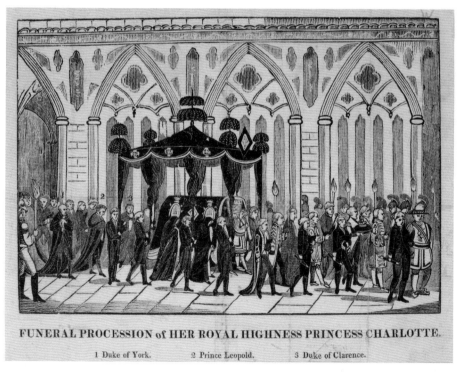

FUNERAL PROCESSION of HER ROYAL HIGHNESS PRINCESS CHARLOTTE.

1 Duke of York.　　2 Prince Leopold.　　3 Duke of Clarence.

Princess Charlotte's funeral procession, with the dukes of York and Clarence, together with the newly widowed Prince Leopold. (Philadelphia Museum of Art, the Muriel and Philip Berman Gift. Accession Number: 1985-52-7095)

Charlotte, who brought up her royal brood of fifteen children there, but it lacked decent heating and sanitation and was considered sub-standard for the new king. Parliament were aghast at the profligacy of their monarch as he poured hundreds of thousands of pounds into the project – and the taxpayers were similarly furious that the burden of the extravagance fell on them. In 1827 Carlton House was finally demolished. Many of the architectural details were dismantled and incorporated into Buckingham Palace, along with much of the furniture and art works. Ironically, the work was never finished in his lifetime and neither George IV nor his brother William IV ever lived there.

Nowadays the building most associated with the Prince Regent is the Royal Pavilion at Brighton. George had first visited the town because his dissolute uncle had a holiday home there and George preferred the rakish atmosphere of Brighton to the somewhat staid company of his father at Weymouth. Initially he rented a small farmhouse in the town, but in 1787 he started work on building the extraordinary royal residence which became the Brighton Pavilion, with construction being spread over thirty-five years. It started out modestly enough,

Detail from roofline of the Royal Pavilion at Brighton. (Author's collection)

in the neo-classical style. Successive waves of building, latterly under the auspices of John Nash, produced a striking building with influences from China, India, and goodness knows where else. It was still a popular residence when William IV succeeded his brother George IV to the throne, but fell out of favour with Queen Victoria who hated the place. It remains as a frothy creation made of many styles, a monument to the extraordinary taste and willingness to encompass new ideas of a man dismissed when he died with the words: 'There never was an individual less regretted by his fellow-creatures than this deceased king.' Those words appeared in *The Times* of 15 July 1830, but they fail to give credit for the huge boost he gave to architecture, painting, literature and music through his support and patronage. His extravagance may have made him unpopular, his hypocrisy may have caused resentment, but at least he was never boring.

2

WAR, POLITICS AND CIVIL UNREST

In 1800 Britain was already seven years into an expensive and resource-consuming war with France. It was a struggle not just to be top dog in Europe, but for worldwide naval supremacy. Ultimately, Britain's success led to colonial domination and the rapid expansion of the British Empire. By 1802 the combatants had fought themselves into something of a standstill and the Treaty of Amiens was signed. The British public wanted peace – and, with it, an end to the Income Tax which had been imposed in order to meet the country's liabilities and to reduce the National Debt. People flocked to cross the Channel, including the Whig politician Charles Fox, the artist Turner, the poet Wordsworth, the diarist Frances Burney and the astronomer William Herschel, all anxious to resume contact with their French friends. Suddenly French wines and fashions could be imported into the country, but not for long. The peace lasted just one year. Neither side had been willing to implement all of the terms of the treaty in full, and mistrust of Napoleon on the part of the British was matched by the Emperor's view that Britain had no right to say what could, or could not, happen on the continent of Europe. Many English tourists were trapped in Paris and, unable to return home when hostilities broke out in May 1803 and Napoleon prepared to invade Britain. In turn, the Russians and Austrians were preparing to invade France. Napoleon won crushing victories at Ulm and Austerlitz over the forces threatening France. However, the English victory at Trafalgar in October 1805, inspired by the leadership of Nelson, ensured that the British navy was able to continue blockading its French counterpart into ports such as Brest for most of the remainder of the war. The death of Nelson at Trafalgar was followed by a period of national mourning, the body lying in state at Greenwich before being escorted to Westminster Abbey under the mournful eyes of no fewer than 10,000 soldiers.

Whereas the British navy dominated at sea, the French armies were almost invincible on land. Napoleon's forces defeated coalition after coalition raised

'England expects that every man will do his duty in 1805.' This picture, by Laurie & Whittle, marked the death of Nelson. (Courtesy of CPW)

against them. The tide started to turn in the Spanish Peninsular War, where Wellesley joined the Spanish guerrilla fighters opposing the French forces which had invaded Spain in 1807. Wellesley succeeded in driving the French out of Portugal and, after years of largely inconclusive fighting, won victories at Ciudad Rodrigo, Badajoz, and Salamanca. French troops were finally forced out of Spain during the winter of 1813–14. This war in Spain had cost Napoleon dearly, tying up troops and hampering his plans to deliver a knockout blow against the Russians. In the event, his *Grande Armée* of 650,000 men had marched on Moscow in 1812, but when Napoleon's forces entered the city, they found that the Russian army had simply abandoned their capital and declined to negotiate. Napoleon was forced to retreat; his army were desperately short of food and supplies and totally ill-equipped for the rigours of the Russian winter.

By the time the *Grande Armée* left Russian soil at the end of 1812 only 27,000 fit men remained. Nearly half a million soldiers had died, been captured or were seriously injured. In time, allied forces drove Napoleon back, capturing Paris in 1814 and forcing Napoleon to abdicate. He was exiled to Elba and, believing that war in Europe was nearly over, the European leaders convened the Congress of Vienna. It represented an attempt to draw up a new map of Europe, balancing the powers of continental giants such as France, Prussia, Austria and Russia. Back in Britain, the Prince Regent wished to bask in the reflected glory of a French defeat, commissioning Thomas Lawrence to paint a series of portraits of the victorious leaders to be hung at Carlton House. In the event, the celebration was premature as Napoleon escaped from Elba, rebuilt his army, and marched on Brussels to face the combined forces of Wellington and Blücher. The forces met at Waterloo on 18 June 1815.

That day some 55,000 men were either killed, wounded or went missing in action, with thousands requiring immediate medical attention (usually amputations) on the battlefield. The scale of death and mutilation was horrific and, paraphrasing Wellington, it was 'a damn close-run thing.' The result was a final defeat for the French; Napoleon had indeed 'met his Waterloo'. He went into exile again, this time to far-off St Helena.

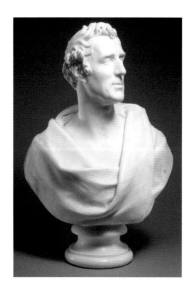 

Above left: Arthur Wellesley (1769–1852), 1st Duke of Wellington, by Sir Francis Chantrey. (Metropolitan Museum of Art, Wrightsman Fund. Accession Number: 1994.295a, b)

Above right: 'Waterloo Studies.' (Yale Center for British Art)

'Battle of Waterloo', showing the defeated Napoleon leaving the field of battle on his white charger. (Library of Congress, LC-USZC2-1969)

Defeat of the French meant that the Prince Regent could expand his plans for an artistic commemoration. More leaders were added to the list of portraits to be painted by Lawrence, and this time they would all be hung in the Waterloo Room, specially constructed at Windsor Castle. In 1827 the triumphal Marble Arch, built to the design of John Nash, was erected at Buckingham Palace in order to form a grand entrance to the *cour d'honneur* – the three-sided courtyard intended to impress visitors and to remind them of the achievements of the former Prince Regent, by now crowned George IV. It was only when Queen Victoria came to the throne and decided to build a fourth side to Buckingham Palace that the Marble Arch was dismantled and re-erected on its present site.

Domestic politics were dominated in the opening years of the Regency period by William Pitt the Younger. He had always enjoyed the support of George III, whereas the Prince of Wales had traditionally been a supporter of the Whig firebrand Charles James Fox. Fox was finally invited into the government as part of the Ministry of All the Talents, which was formed in 1806 after the death of Pitt. It was intended to be a national unity government under the leadership of Baron Grenville. In the event, the Ministry of All the Talents had little success, particularly in its desire to bring about peace in Europe. War rumbled on for a further decade and the ministry fell apart over disagreements about Catholic Emancipation. In its place the Duke of Portland became Prime Minister for the second time (he had held office twenty-four years earlier). He headed a fractious group of former Pitt supporters, which included George Canning and Lord Castlereagh. These two were constantly at loggerheads, preventing any effective government. Matters came to a head when Castlereagh, then Secretary of War and the Colonies, challenged Canning (Foreign Secretary) to a duel. It took place on Putney Heath in September 1809, and resulted in Canning being shot in the thigh. The public were appalled that two cabinet ministers should take matters so far. The Prime Minister was in poor health and opted to part company from his feuding ministers. When Portland resigned in 1809 his place was taken by Spencer Perceval.

Perceval was an unusual character – he described himself not as a Tory but as 'a friend of Mr Pitt'. He was opposed to gambling, adultery and heavy drinking. He opposed hunting and slavery, as well as the giving of voting rights to Roman Catholics. He favoured the continuation of the war with France, and it was while he was in office that the Regency crisis came to a head. George III was becoming increasingly mentally unstable and the old Regency Bill was dusted off and again put before Parliament. Perceval wanted Queen Charlotte to be involved in looking after the king, and to have a panel of trustees appointed to look after the king's personal property. He also wanted to curb the powers of patronage which would otherwise pass to the Prince of Wales as Regent. Perceval harboured deep suspicions about the Whig sympathies of the Prince of Wales, fearing that he would undermine the monarchy and encourage republicanism. He accordingly proposed a moratorium on the creation of new peers by the Regent, and a suspension of rights to award pensions and official posts. These restrictions were to last for twelve months. Despite this obvious friction between the prince and the prime minister, the Regency Bill was steered through Parliament in February 1811. The restrictions expired a year later and, much to everyone's surprise, the Regent did not sack Perceval or insist on a change of government. Perceval was a skilful politician, but not one who benefited financially from high office. For his troubles he was shot in May 1812 in the lobby of the House of Commons. Perceval died almost immediately, leaving behind a wife and twelve young children, and barely one hundred pounds to his name. His assailant was a man called Bellingham, who was aggrieved that the government had not awarded him compensation when he had been imprisoned in Russia some years before. He

Painting by George Munger showing the ruins of the U.S. Capitol following British attempts to burn the building, with damage to the Senate and House wings, and the shell of the rotunda with the facade and roof missing. (Library of Congress, DRWG/US – Munger)

was tried at the Old Bailey, found guilty, and executed on 18 May, exactly one week after the shooting.

War with Napoleon was not the only Regency conflict. In 1812 hostilities broke out between Britain and the newly formed United States, in the course of which British forces sacked and burned the White House and sought to impose a sea blockade along the eastern seaboard. The American plan to expand its interests into Canada was thwarted, but in 1815 American forces under General Jackson defeated a British scheme to capture New Orleans. Back in Britain, the public became fed up with having to pay taxes to cover the cost of conflict in America, and merchants in cities such as Bristol and Liverpool wished to resume their Atlantic trading activities. Peace was brought about with the Treaty of Ghent, which involved no changes to the pre-war boundaries, but which laid the foundations for far better trading connections across the Atlantic. What was known as the 1818 Treaty, and the Rush–Bagot Treaty of the same year, effectively demilitarised the Great Lakes area, and established the 49th Parallel as the international boundary between America and Canada.

In the domestic arena, the Regency period saw a number of highly significant changes, starting with the Union with Ireland on 1 January 1801. The Act of

A naval encounter from the War of 1812 showing the US sloop *Wasp* seeking to board the frigate HMS *Frolic*. (Museum of Philadelphia, gift of the McNeil Americana Collection. Accession Number: 2011-91-3)

Union combined the two Kingdoms, as well as uniting the two Parliaments. Initially it was intended to lead to Catholic emancipation, but George III was opposed to any attempt to allow the Roman Catholics to vote, or to stand for Parliament, and it was not until 1829 that this situation changed. Up until that date only Anglican MPs could be elected to the Irish Parliament, despite the fact that the population was mostly Catholic. The actual Act of Union in Ireland was passed after a good deal of bribery and corruption, and the delay in implementing electoral reform caused great unrest. In England, the problems of lack of electoral representation were exacerbated by the rapid growth of cities such as Manchester and Leeds. The people felt that they had no voice and wished to see parliamentary reform, but this was opposed by many in Parliament, especially those who represented 'rotten boroughs', which were in effect in the pockets of just one or two local families. At St Peter's Field in Manchester on 16 August 1819 a crowd gathered to listen to the political radical Henry Hunt. Magistrates panicked and called in the troops. When cavalry charged the assembled crowds, sabres drawn, carnage followed with fifteen people killed and hundreds wounded. The incident became known as the Peterloo Massacre (an ironic reference to the victory at Waterloo four years earlier). In its wake Parliament passed the Six Acts, the most important one being the Seditious Meetings Act which made illegal any gathering of more than fifty persons to discuss any political subject unless the prior permission had been obtained either from the magistrate or the sheriff. Minor reforms to voting rights were enacted, but the groundswell of a demand for greater suffrage was not met until just after the end of the Regency period, when the Great Reform Act was passed in 1832. In the meantime the political scene was dominated by the Tories who vehemently opposed reform. Especially after Peterloo, anyone seeking greater suffrage was likely to be treated as a revolutionary, and with the example of the French very much in everybody's minds, the Tory establishment was increasingly repressive. Under Lord Liverpool, in office between 1815 and 1827, there was little chance of legislation to reform Parliament being enacted.

The Regency was a period marked by civil disturbances. After the end of the Napoleonic Wars unemployment soared as soldiers were laid off and employers tried to benefit by driving down wages. This coincided with a shortage of food, leading to widespread unrest. Many people felt threatened by the mechanisation which characterised this period of the Industrial Revolution. Labourers found themselves out of work and often resorted to violence and rioting to express their dissatisfaction. The Luddites, named after a (probably fictitious) character called Ned Ludd, were responsible for smashing up power looms and spinning frames in textile factories between 1811 and 1817. In 1812 the Malicious Damage Act and the Frame Breaking Act had been passed, making machine-breaking a capital offence. Later, the Swing Riots of 1830 saw agricultural workers protest at the new threshing machines which were driving them from their jobs on the land.

Conditions for the poor worsened with the passing of the 1815 Corn Law. This protectionist piece of legislation, aimed at benefiting wealthy landowners by imposing a hefty tariff on imported grains, meant that grain prices stayed high. Bread was no longer affordable for the urban and agricultural poor. The situation was exacerbated when Mount Tambora in Indonesia exploded in 1816. Dust thrown high into the atmosphere encircled the globe, causing what became known as the 'year without summer'. Crops failed, and livestock starved to death. The freedom of workers to form themselves into trade unions had been prohibited by the Combination Act of 1799 and the huge inequality of bargaining power between landowners and individual employees caused great resentment, which spilled over into the reign of William IV. Many of the itinerant poor were caught by the provisions of the Vagrancy Act of 1824, which gave magistrates the power

Thomas Rowlandson's 'Harvesters Resting in a Corn Field', from around 1805. (Yale Center for British Art, Paul Mellon Collection. Accession Number: B198.29.469)

to order the detention of 'vagabonds and incorrigible rogues'. Indeed they faced being whipped and sentenced to hard labour. A new Treason Act, changes to the law of habeas corpus, and a new Criminal Libel Act all appeared on the statute book in the Regency period, all aimed at controlling the rights of individuals.

One of the calls of those who were opposed to the abolition of slavery was that the country should do more to look after its own poor and not worry about the plight of slaves thousands of miles away. Nevertheless the efforts of men like Thomas Clarkson and William Wilberforce led to the actual trade in slaves being made illegal in 1808. It was perhaps the most important achievement of the Ministry of All the Talents, mentioned earlier. The battle for hearts and minds continued throughout the Regency period, although slavery itself was not abolished until 1833 when the Slavery Act was passed, three days before the death of Wilberforce.

3

SOCIETY AND
THE SOCIAL SCENE

It was an era when birth and rank were of paramount importance, and the pecking order was rigidly enforced to ensure that privilege remained with the privileged – royalty, aristocracy, gentry, middle class, and others down the line.

The nobility consisted of the family of a duke/duchess, marquis/marchioness, earl/countess, viscount/viscountess, or baron/baroness. Traditionally, the eldest son of an aristocrat inherited the estates, while other brothers, unless lucky enough to have an inheritance or allowance to support them, would join the army, the navy, the diplomatic service or take up politics. Alternatively they could be given an ecclesiastical living on the family estate. The gentry were landowners, baronets, knights, esquires and gentlemen (a gentleman was a man of independent means, i.e. he did not have to work). The middle classes (known as the 'Middling Sort') were very diverse, and included doctors, lawyers, factory owners, bankers, and merchants, as well as yeoman farmers, craftsmen, shopkeepers and school teachers. Middle-class boundaries were constantly shifting according to wealth and education, and often merged with the lower gentry. 'Nabobs' were men who had returned from India having made a fortune, while a 'chicken nabob' had made a smaller fortune. Nabobs were often black sheep who had been sent away, or middle-class, well-educated youths without expectations. Some returned ill and penniless, but many returned to save their families financially, or buy their own estates. Other ranks in the social hierarchy included artisans, trades-people, servants, labourers and paupers.

The hedonistic and extravagant lifestyle pursued by many of 'the Quality' was unsustainable over time (especially where gambling was involved) and many noble families became heavily over-extended. If penniless sons could not find a noble heiress, they would need to marry the daughter of a wealthy cit – a rescue package which continued long after the Regency. A cit (as in 'the city') was a member of the wealthy middle class, often self-made. Whereas they could not achieve social elevation themselves they could aspire to it through their daughters, by effectively buying a title.

'Monstrosities of 1799' by James Gillray. (Lewis Walpole Library)

'Monstrosities of 1822' by George Cruikshank. (Library of Congress, Call Number PC 1 - 14438)

Marriage was usually arranged for reasons of fortune (acquiring it, increasing it, or keeping it) or status (lineage, ancestry, titles, property and breeding). Those who could marry for love were few and fortunate. Dynastic marriages were the norm, and the eldest son was expected to marry and provide an heir. Children (however old) were not expected to disoblige their family aspirations, heiresses especially. They were expected to marry a greater title than their own, and were zealously guarded from unsuitable fortune hunters, however charming.

Ambitious mothers would launch their daughters into 'the Marriage Mart' seeking to gain wealth or status – or hopefully both. Marriage was simply an imperative for most young women, because without a husband they could not hope to find security, and, unless they were in the lower orders, employment was simply not an option. To be a governess was socially inferior, and in any event many women lacked the education needed for this or any other employment.

Gentlemen usually belonged to a club – White's, Brooks's and Watier's were pre-eminent – in order to meet friends, socialise in the evenings and indulge in playing cards or dice for money. Gaming also took place at private houses but this was not always reputable. Betting was an obsession with fashionable young men and was applied to almost all the activities they either watched or engaged in, from horse-racing, boxing, fencing and shooting, right down to cock-fighting. Hunting was popular, and well-heeled gentlemen might own a hunting box in the shires, where they would keep a stable of horses. Most sought-after was membership of hunts such as the Quorn and the Belvoir. Driving was fashionable, especially with phaetons and curricles, and there was no higher accolade than to be known as a notable whip. When in town, gentleman (and ladies who were à la mode) would ride or drive at the fashionable hour of the five o'clock promenade, and Rotten Row was particularly popular. Each city had its own stylish venue. It was a time to see and be seen, whether walking, or on horseback, or in a carriage.

It was almost customary for gentleman to keep a mistress, and the leading courtesans were known as the Toast of the Town. Their lover was expected to provide them with jewellery, expensive clothes and often an apartment. Top ranking courtesans would have their own box at the opera and theatre, a luxury which could cost over £2,000 for the season. It was modish to take supper after the theatre at somewhere such as the Piazza, or to visit Vauxhall Gardens (for music and masquerades).

Other popular entertainment venues were Astley's Amphitheatre (the circus) and the Surrey (burlettas). During the day, well-bred ladies would pass the time shopping, paying or receiving calls, or with a hobby such as playing the fortepiano, painting

'Dandies in Rotten Row' by G. M. Woodward. (Lewis Walpole Library)

in watercolours, or embroidery. In the evening they would indulge in dancing, or attend assemblies and balls. The ability to dance was an essential accomplishment for both men and women, because it was almost the only way of forming or cementing a connection. Gentlemen would need to be introduced to a lady before inviting her to dance. Dances would be reserved in advance, and there was no greater accolade than to have all one's dances reserved on a lady's dance card. Less fortunate maidens would have to sit aside with their chaperone or companion, unless solicited.

The usual dances were the quadrille, the cotillion and the country dance (contredanse) which were set pattern dances with multiple couples. The waltz was originally stigmatised as 'fast' or improper because a single gentleman and lady danced alone, with the gentleman holding the lady. However, the waltz was both fashionable and accepted by 1815. Almacks was still at the pinnacle of the social scene. Although very sedate, with only limited refreshments available, it provided suppers and dancing for social aspirants. If you could not get in to Almacks you were not fully in society, and admission was controlled by a tight group of patronesses. Money alone could not buy entry.

The social scene for the wealthy and titled, influenced by the Regent, was all about etiquette, manners and status. Whether in town (London) for the Season, or taking the waters (Bath, Cheltenham or Tunbridge Wells) or visiting the seaside (Brighton) or their country estates, the elaborate rituals of polite society would be observed. Receiving or paying 'morning calls' (often in the afternoon), the need to be introduced before starting a conversation, and giving precedence to those of a higher rank were all vitally important. The expression 'the ton' – shortened from the French 'haut ton' – was used to describe people of high fashion or birth. An alternative expression was the beau monde (literally, 'the beautiful world'). 'Ton' could also be used to indicate taste, or form, as in 'good ton', meaning to be well-bred and to have 'a certain something', or 'bad ton' in other words ill-bred, for example if one failed to honour their gambling debts.

It was important to be part of the Season when society gathered in London to engage in the social whirl. The main purpose of the Season was to meet all the right people and to form all the right connections, usually with a view to marriage, as well as to provide considerably more enjoyment and diversion than could be found in the country. The exact timing of the season is harder to define. To begin with it was a period coinciding with the sessions of Parliament – when the movers and shakers in society had come down to London to attend parliamentary (and their own) business. Originally it started in late October and continued until Parliament entered the summer recess, in June. But the dates were not set in stone, and parliamentary terms altered so that by 1822 sittings did not start until February and continued into the summer. In general though, 'the Season' meant avoiding London altogether during the hotter summer months, when the air was considered fetid and unhealthy. The height of the Season was taken as being the period immediately after Easter – all of the royal family would

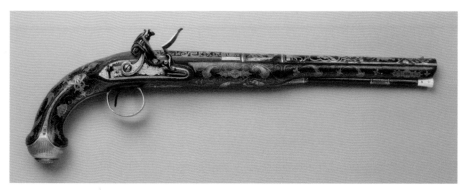

A flintlock pistol from 1811. Although duelling was illegal, whether with pistols or swords, it was still used as a method of settling disputes where honour was at stake. (Philadelphia Museum of Art, bequest of Carl Otto Kretzschmar von Kienbusch. Accession Number: 1977-167-865b)

be back in residence, and this was the period for the most fashionable balls and soirees, and presentations at court. Young ladies needed to be presented to the queen by an affluent relative before formally entering 'society' (known as 'coming out') and young gentlemen would be sponsored at an all-male levee at St James's, attended by the Prince Regent.

When in London the aristocracy would open up their town mansions, the gentry would hire houses in suitably fashionable areas, like Mayfair, and young men would live in lodgings such as the Albany. The lifestyle of the aristocracy (and the wealthy emerging middle classes) was supported by a host of servants who also had their own complex hierarchy, from the steward down to the humble footman or kitchen maid. Retainers and those in service often stayed with the same families for entire lifetimes and across generations – they would be housed, clothed and fed, but hours would be long and duties onerous.

The wealthy derived their income principally from rents on land and property, as well as from investments. The London Stock Exchange was established by 1802. The 'funds' paid a safe return of between 3 and 5 per cent, and 'consols' (government bonds) were popular. An income of £10,000 would be more than enough to support a great country estate and a London town house, plus all the staff and trimmings – a very comfortable life-style enjoyed by the privileged few. It is the income mentioned by Jane Austen as being enjoyed by Mr Darcy. Mr Bingley, with only half that amount, was still extremely well-off.

One particular feature of the Regency was the rise of the dandy (otherwise known as the Exquisite). To begin with, dandyism was not a particularly pejorative term, being associated with cleanliness, well-pressed clothing and a

Gentlemen's Carriages: A Cabriolet, painted by Charles Hancock between 1820 and 1830. (Yale Center for British Art, Paul Mellon Collection)

fastidious attention to detail. In time it became associated with a particularly effeminate style of dress, with satirists ridiculing the exponents of dandy fashion such as 'Poodle Byng' (the Honourable Frederick Gerald Byng) and 'Golden Ball' (the nickname for Edward Hughes Ball Hughes). William Arden, 2nd Baron Alvanley, was a hugely popular, good natured and handsome dandy, with a reputation for dressing immaculately.

The term 'Beau' denoted a fashionable person who was accepted as an arbiter of good taste, and was applied to a man with presence, though not necessarily good looks. A 'Corinthian' was a sportsman who dressed well and could mix with both his peers and the sporting fraternity, whether at a boxing match, fencing or driving his curricle ('tooling his carriage'). The highest accolade was awarded to the cream of the aesthetes, the fashion-setter and the man everyone deferred to: he would be termed the 'Nonpareil' or 'Nonesuch'. A 'fop' was a derogatory word used to describe an overly ostentatious fellow who tried to attract attention by his extreme sense of fashion – such as the wearing of absurdly high collars, which prevented the wearer from turning his head. 'Bucks' were invariably the younger members of noble families with independent means. They would be turned out 'in the current mode' and their conduct was often associated with frivolity and irresponsible, sometimes dangerous, behaviour.

A scene in a club lounge, by Thomas Rowlandson, showing members and attendants sitting, dozing and eating. (Brown University)

4

FASHION

An inordinate amount of time and attention was spent by both genders in dressing and in personal presentation, often changing three or four times a day into the 'correct' attire. Fashions changed constantly, the only consistent factor was the need to keep up with the latest trends, and magazines such as *La Belle Assemblée* and *Ackermann's Repository* were full of colour plates and information about what was in vogue.

LADIES' FASHIONS

The shape of women evolved in the Regency era, with high-waisted dresses (tight under the bust), low cut bodices and puff sleeves being the norm. Gradually, after 1820 the waistline started to drop, reaching 'normal' by the 1830s. For daytime modesty a lady might wear either a fichu or a tucker to hide her décolletage. This was particularly important in the morning, when very little flesh would be exposed. Afternoon dresses were less demure, and therefore allowed greater freedom of movement. Fabrics in general use included muslin (a corruption of the word 'Muslim', denoting its Middle Eastern origins) and this could be plain or patterned. Sometimes the muslin was so diaphanous as to be almost see-through, especially when damp. Crepe, sarsanet, cambric and dimity were also popular, but married women were more likely to wear silks and satins. Dresses were full length, often buttoned all the way down to the ankles, and frequently elaborately trimmed with scallops, braids, knots or ribbons. Exotic trimmings such as swans down became fashionable.

Hats were an essential item, with fashions changing every year, leading to eccentricities such as beehive bonnets, villager hats, the poke bonnet, or turbans. Milliners in London catered to all tastes, however extreme, and hats could be very expensive. Young ladies presented at court were required to sport ostrich plumes. Poorer households would make do with adorning simple bonnets with ribbons,

Above left: 'Fashionable Furbeloes', a cartoon published by S. W. Fores in 1801. Furbelow was the name for showy ornamental ruffles or flounces. (Lewis Walpole Library)

Above right: Poke bonnet. (Rijkmuseum)

bows, flowers and feathers. Straw hats were generally favoured in summer, while velvet or silk was popular in the winter. Older women would tend to wear lace caps indoors. A calash was a bonnet resembling the hooped top of a carriage and was worn well into the Victorian era.

Accessories included parasols, leather gloves, reticules (which were like purses), silk stockings, and shawls especially made of zephyr (a very fine light cotton) or Norwich silk, or cashmere (originally from Kashmir). Buttons, braids, spangles and elaborate trimmings were the order of the day, with extravagant jewellery being worn by the wealthy at formal occasions – tiaras, aigrettes, drop earrings and necklaces.

Fans remained popular at balls and assemblies, and were usually beautifully carved or decorated. The most sought-after fans were made using a technique

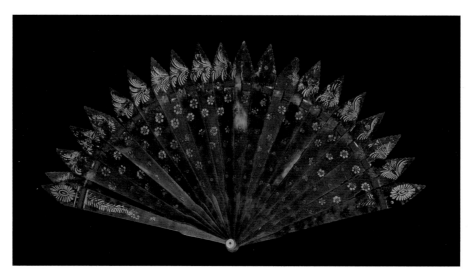

Brisé fan made of tortoiseshell and mother-of-pearl. (Brooklyn Museum Costume Collection at the Metropolitan Museum of Art. Accession Number: 2009.300.4026)

called Vernis Martin, and were hand-painted and lacquered. Pleated fans might be made of silk, frosted crepe, or chicken skin. Brisé fans could be made out of tortoise shell, ivory or mother-of-pearl.

The continuing war with France led to a vogue for wearing clothing with a military theme, such as the ubiquitous pelisse. This was a coat-style overdress, which could be either full- or calf-length, often designed to allow a view of the gown underneath. The coat would be worn for warmth over a flimsy but fashionable muslin dress, and was often buttoned down from neck to hem. It usually followed the empire line by being tight under the bust. In extreme weather a pilgrim's cloak or shoulder cape would be added, while wealthy married ladies would sport furs. An alternative was the Spencer, a jacket which finished just below the bust. It was a high-necked, long-sleeved garment which could be embellished with stylish points or a neck ruff, and was often made of velvet for extra warmth. A different sort of coat was the full-length, fitted redingote, popular towards the end of the Regency. It had a wide flat collar, and overlapped before fastening across the chest. It was generally made of wool.

Fashions distinguished between dresses worn in the morning (which were often made of figured muslin or dimity) and afternoon dresses (including walking dresses, which were fuller and heavier, often featuring fine Merino wool). A lady could also have a separate carriage dress, which, by the time of

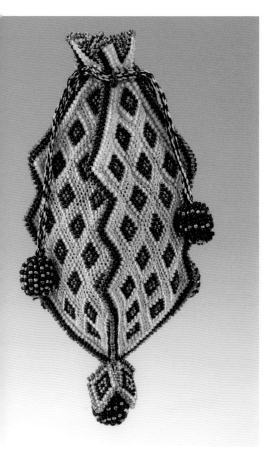

Above left: Reticule. (Brooklyn Museum Costume Collection at the Metropolitan Museum of Art. Accession Number: 2009.300.1902)

Above right: Silk pelisse from 1820. (Brooklyn Museum Costume Collection at the Metropolitan Museum of Art. Accession Number: 2009.300.629)

the Battle of Waterloo, would frequently have a military motif. Fashionable women favoured riding habits, a two-piece costume consisting of a tight-fitting jacket, often decorated with frogging, epaulettes and braiding, and a long skirt which would allow the wearer to ride side-saddle. This might be topped off with a tall hat in the style of a military shako, adorned with feathers. The ensemble would typically be completed with a muslin cravat, lace ruffles, kid gloves and half-length boots. Ladies would always change again for the evening – dressing for dinner was absolutely essential for the well-to-do, and for the aspiring middle classes.

Evenings were an opportunity for extravagance. Beneath the domino (a hooded cloak worn to a masquerade) or the opera cloak a lady might wear a dress consisting of an overdress and underdress. The underdress would be simple and often made of muslin or silk, and the overdress would be more striking, often of lace, spider-gauze, net or embroidered silk. Gloves would be worn above the elbow, along with satin slippers. Shoes were still interchangeable (left and right) since separate lasts were not in general use before 1850.

Court dress was different to normal apparel. Rules of dress laid down by Queen Charlotte remained in force until 1820. These meant that a debutante (a young lady making her debut into Society) would be required to spend many hundreds of pounds on an elaborate but outmoded gown with hoops, which might only be worn once.

Mourning dress was a requirement, with rigid rules according to the degree of closeness to the deceased. 'Putting on black gloves' was a synonym for going into mourning, which could last for anything between six and twelve months. Bombazine, a black fabric made from wool and silk with a matt surface, was particularly favoured. Total black gave way to dove grey, and finally to lavender, as the wearer emerged from mourning, and there were strict rules as to where a woman could go, and what she could do, while she was in mourning.

In place of the fashion for wigs of the previous century, hair was worn more naturally, with side ringlets and top ringlets in vogue. If ringlets did not suit the wearer, there were also classic styles where plaits were taken onto the crown. The more daring might favour the masculine short crop 'à la Sappho'.

Above left: Silk-and-leather evening slippers from 1806. (Brooklyn Museum Costume Collection at the Metropolitan Museum of Art. Accession Number: 2001.576a, b)

Above right: Leather boots used for riding and driving. (Brooklyn Museum Costume Collection at the Metropolitan Museum of Art. Accession Number: 2009.300.1486a, b)

Lady Maria Conyngham, painted in 1825 by Sir Thomas Lawrence. (Metropolitan Museum of art. Gift of Jessie Woolworth Donahue. Accession Number: 55.89)

MEN'S FASHIONS

It is easy to think of Regency styles for men in terms of the influence of George Bryan 'Beau' Brummell – even though in practice he fell from favour in 1816 after being rude to the Prince Regent ('Alvanley, who's your fat friend?'). Regency style was characterised by fastidious attention to detail – it was essential to be 'precise to a pin' (otherwise known as having a 'point-device' appearance). There were two variants of day-time dress: country or riding, and town dress. Country dress involved breeches or buckskins, the latter being most comfortable for riding because they had no inside seam. They were made of deer-suede of a greyish-yellow colour. Breeches could be leather, wool, nankeen or corduroy and would be worn with top boots. The most famous boot maker was George Hoby, who also supplied gentlemen with hessians and evening pumps. For town wear, pantaloons had been the norm in the early Regency but in time were replaced by trousers, not least when the Regent favoured trousers because they disguised his bloated legs. Pantaloons were knitted, skin-tight and usually of pale colours such as buff, biscuit or yellow, and were known as 'inexpressibles'. Trousers were long like pantaloons, but were cut wide at the ankle and were worn with shoes or half-boots, whereas the pantaloons were always worn with hessians – highly polished boots with a 'V' at the knee, and tassels below. Loose, cossack-style trousers drawn in at the ankle were called Petershams (after Lord Petersham), and there was a brief fashion for striped trousers around 1825, when they were much ridiculed by caricaturists.

Jackets were the same whether for country or town wear, and were generally 'swallow-tailed', until 1816 and the introduction of the frock coat. Any gentleman wishing to be à la mode would have his jackets made by one of four tailors: Weston, Schweitzer and Davidson, Stulz, or Scott. Colours were always dark, and fabrics included superfine and kerseymere. When outdoors, a gentleman would wear a topcoat (known as a great coat or Benjamin) which was ankle length and usually made of drab – a thick durable cloth of a dull colour, such as light olive or grey. When driving a carriage he would use a box coat, the most fashionable of which had layers of capes to keep out the rain.

Shirts were usually simple, of cambric or cotton, and both the collar and neck-cloth (cravat) were separate from the shirt. Aspirants to fashion would starch the collars into high points. The tying of the cravat had been elevated to an art form by Beau Brummell, and there were complicated alternatives such as the Waterfall, the Mathematical and the Osbaldeston. A more casual knotted

Lord Leveson-Gower by Thomas Lawrence. (Yale Center for British Art. B1981.25.736)

Lord Petersham, wearing Hessian boots, by Thomas Rowlandson. Petersham was a renowned leader of fashion who gave his name to a hat, a coat and a form of trousers. (Yale Center for British Art)

neck-cloth was termed a Belcher, and was much favoured by gentlemen of a romantic persuasion. It was brightly coloured and named after the boxer Jem Belcher. The stock – a stiff band reinforced with paste-board – was favoured by the armed forces and by the clergy (where it remains to this day in the form of the 'dog collar').

By the Regency period waistcoats were sleeveless, cut so as to be visible at the front under the jacket. Understated elegance meant that waistcoat fabrics were often self-patterned. More brash waistcoats such as the daytime use of florid or ornate materials were regarded as vulgar but that did not stop men wearing spots, stripes or patterns. Evening waistcoats were never coloured.

Gentlemen of a rotund figure (such as the Prince Regent) would wear stays, a form of lace-up corset. Known as a Cumberland, they creaked as the wearer moved. Less-endowed followers of fashion would disguise their lack of musculature with buckram padding worn at the shoulders, and with 'falsies' worn on the calf and thigh.

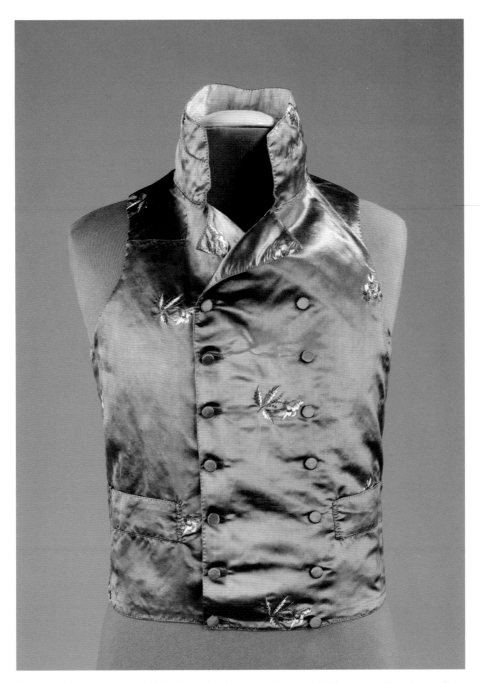

Gentleman's waistcoat *c.* 1810. (Brooklyn Museum Costume Collection at the Metropolitan Museum of Art. Accession Number: 2009.300.2841)

'An Exquisite' by George Cruikshank, dated 1817. (The Elisha Whittelsey Collection, Metropolitan Museum of Art. Accession Number: 1970.541.121.)

Hats of one sort or another were always worn, and the fashionable had them made by either Lock & Co or Baxters. In the early Regency, the hat of choice was the beaver, but in time this gave way to the tall hat, made of a fabric called plush. Beavers were high crowned, with curled brims, and were often grey or fawn. Hair was expected to look effortless, although this effect often took hours to achieve, as with The Windswept and The Brutus. Others favoured the shorter, simpler, Corinthian Crop or the New Dash.

Evening dress consisted of a long-tailed coat with a white waistcoat, black or white satin knee breeches, silk stockings and pumps. People wishing to attend Almacks were required to wear full evening dress, otherwise they were not allowed in. Striped stockings were in vogue, and full evening dress included wearing the *chapeau bras* – a flat bicorne silk hat, typically carried under the arm. Men's court dress was again from a previous era. It was very elaborate and involved carrying a dress sword.

Accessories would include the quizzing glass, worn on a ribbon round the neck, and fobs and pocket watches worn with a gold chain. A cane, usually made from Malacca or ebony, was de rigeur, and might sometimes convert into a sword-stick. Gloves (usually pigskin) were worn by gentlemen, and they would invariably carry a snuffbox, often intricately engraved or enamelled, and no doubt filled with snuff from Fribourg and Treyer, snuff-makers to the Royal family. Discreet nosegays would be worn in button holes, except for members of the Four Horse Club who traditionally wore extravagant nosegays, along with a waistcoat with blue and yellow stripes, and a white muslin cravat with black spots.

5

LITERATURE AND
THE ENGLISH NOVEL

The Romantic movement, which can be traced back to the works of Goethe in Germany in the 1770s and which gained a big boost after the events in Revolutionary France, blossomed in Britain in the Regency period. What was romanticism? It was in part a reaction to the Industrial Revolution, and a move away from the idea that everything could be rationalised and explained. In place of control and order, artists, writers and musicians brought emotions and passion to the fore. Their works were about sensitivity and feelings, and emphasised fear, terror, and sadness, but also elation and wonderment. Whether it was the artist Blake painting hideous representations of Hell, or writing tormented poetry about oppression and tyranny, or Wordsworth extolling the beauty of nature in his beloved Lake District, or Byron, the ultimate romantic hero, with his epic narrative poem 'Childe Harold's Pilgrimage', emotions were brought out into the open. Mystery and horror were explored in Mary Shelley's *Frankenstein*, alternatively known as *The Modern Prometheus*. Her novel first appeared in print in 1818, anonymously, and although it met with disapproval from many critics it was an instant success with the public. Jane Austen's works may at first sight seem poles apart from a tale of horror and unimaginable terror, but she too explored emotions, especially unrequited love, as well as commenting on the follies and foibles of contemporary society.

It is perhaps in poetry that the Romantic movement found its greatest expression, with Wordsworth and Coleridge at the forefront of the genre. Together they published *Lyrical Ballads* in 1798, with numerous reprints in the early years of the nineteenth century. In a later preface to the work, Wordsworth defined poetry as 'the spontaneous overflow of powerful feelings: it takes its origin from emotion recollected in tranquillity.' His most famous poem, 'I Wandered Lonely as a Cloud' (also commonly known as 'Daffodils'), was published in 1802. Coleridge contributed 'The Rime of the Ancient Mariner' to *Lyrical Ballads* but increasing bouts of depression and opium dependency curtailed his literary output. 'Kubla Khan; or, A Vision in a Dream: A Fragment' was written in 1797 but was left unpublished until 1816. Quoted here is a short extract:

In Xanadu did Kubla Khan
A stately Pleasure-Dome decree,
Where Alph, the sacred river ran
Through caverns measureless to man
Down to a sunless sea.
So twice five miles of fertile ground
With walls and towers were girdled 'round,
And there were gardens bright with sinuous rills,
Where blossom'd many an incense-bearing tree;
And here were forests ancient as the hills,
Enfolding sunny spots of greenery.

The trio of Keats, Shelley and Byron developed romanticism, and all shared a common bond: they all died tragically young.

Keats was twenty-five when he died, and his works had been published only in the final four years of his life. Although his poems met a measure of critical acclaim at the time, it was only after his death in 1821 that his reputation developed. He was eight

Portrait of John Keats by Joseph Severn.
(© National Portrait Gallery, London)

when his father was killed in a riding accident. He was fourteen when his mother died of tuberculosis, and twenty-three when his brother Tom succumbed to the same condition. He himself generally 'enjoyed ill-health' and would eventually die of the same disease. A humble background (his father was an ostler) meant that he never attended Eton or Harrow, or went to Oxbridge. Instead he trained in medicine before giving up that career to concentrate on writing, with 1819 seeing him write several of his famous odes including this excerpt from 'Ode to a Nightingale':

> My heart aches, and a drowsy numbness pains
> My sense, as though of hemlock I had drunk,
> Or emptied some dull opiate to the drains
> One minute past, and Lethe-wards had sunk:
> 'Tis not through envy of thy happy lot,
> But being too happy in thine happiness,
> That thou, light-wingèd Dryad of the trees
> In some melodious plot
> Of beechen green, and shadows numberless,
> Singest of summer in full-throated ease.

He had met and befriended Fanny Brawne in 1817 and wrote many passionate letters to her, but ill-health forced him to move away from her and to seek the warmer climate of Rome. Here, he entered the final phase of what he termed his 'family illness'. Before he died in Rome he had written to Fanny in February 1820, saying 'I have left no immortal work behind me – nothing to make my friends proud of my memory – but I have lov'd the principle of beauty in all things, and if I had had time I would have made myself remember'd.' Seven weeks after Keats died, Shelley wrote 'Adonaïs: An Elegy on the Death of John Keats, Author of Endymion, Hyperion, etc'. His poems inspired the later pre-Raphaelites including Millais and Rossetti, and in time Keats emerged as one of the most influential poets the country has ever produced.

Shelley was a friend and admirer of Keats. He too died young (at the age of twenty-nine, in 1822) and he also never achieved fame or popularity in his own lifetime. His was a life marked by turbulent love affairs, suicides and scandals. He drowned in a boating accident in Italy, while sailing his boat called *Don Juan* (named as a tribute to his friend Lord Byron). His poetry ('The sunlight clasps the earth, and the moonbeams kiss the sea: what are all these kissings worth, if thou kiss not me?') greatly influenced the next generation of poets and essayists, and

Percy Byshhe Shelley by Amelia Curran.
(© National Portrait Gallery, London)

he became particularly associated with non-violent political protest. His radical views had alienated many in his lifetime and indeed many publishers avoided his works fearing that they would be caught up in allegations of blasphemy and sedition. After his death he emerged as one of the country's finest lyric poets.

George Gordon Byron, later known as George Gordon Noel, 6th Baron Byron, was another poet who was cut down in his prime, dying at the age of thirty-six in 1824. But unlike Keats and Shelley, he achieved huge success and fame in his lifetime, becoming an overnight sensation following the publication of the first two cantos of 'Childe Harold's Pilgrimage' in 1812. He had travelled extensively in Europe as part of his Grand Tour, as well as swimming the Hellespont (now, The Dardanelles) linking the Aegean Sea to the Sea of Marmara. When he returned to London in 1811 he became the darling of fashionable society, attending all the best clubs and soirées. But his love-life led to public outrage, with allegations of incest involving his relationship with his half-sister Augusta. He also conducted a scandalous affair with Lady Caroline Lamb, wife of the man who later became Lord Melbourne, Prime Minister. It was Lady Caroline who delivered the best epitaph for the philandering Byron: 'mad, bad, and dangerous to know'.

Heavily in debt, Byron married a wealthy heiress called Annabella Millbanke in 1815. They had a child (Ada) but within a year Annabella started separation proceedings, no doubt fed up with her husband's serial infidelities. For his part, Byron wanted to escape the public scrutiny of his love-life and, in particular, the public abhorrence of his relationship with his half-sister. He left England in 1816, never to return. He moved to Switzerland and then Italy, writing his epic poem 'Don Juan'

Above left: Lord Byron, *c.* 1820. (The Milton Weil Collection at the Metropolitan Museum. Accession Number: 40.20.2)

Above right: Lord Byron. (© National Portrait Gallery, London)

over a number of years between 1818 and 1823. It proved to be extremely popular, although many were shocked by the immorality of its central character who spends much of his time either seducing or being seduced by the women he encounters.

Byron then decided to support the Greek independence movement, as it sought to escape from being ruled as part of the Ottoman Empire. Byron raised funds for the cause, equipping the Greek Navy, and was all set to accompany Greek troops preparing to attack Turkish forces at Lepanto, in the mouth of the Gulf of Corinth. However, he became violently ill. Either in spite of medical treatment, or more likely because of it, he died in April 1824. His embalmed body was brought back to England but the authorities refused to permit a burial at Westminster Abbey on the grounds of his immoral behaviour and bad reputation. Instead he was buried in the Church of St. Mary Magdalene in Hucknall, Nottinghamshire, and it was to be another 145 years before a memorial plaque was finally put up in Westminster Abbey. Byron, like the heroic figures he wrote about, was a flawed but passionate genius, arrogant, rebellious, and not afraid to offend society. Nowadays the words 'Regency' and 'romantic hero' are inescapably linked, thanks to innumerable novels, and in many ways that link exists because of Byron – both in terms of what he wrote, and the reckless way he lived his life.

JANE AUSTEN

It would be hard to imagine a more complete opposite to Lord Byron than Jane Austen, with her shrewd observations on manners and proper behaviour. Jane Austen's first published novel, *Sense and Sensibility*, appeared in 1811 when Jane was thirty-six years old. Her name did not appear on the title page, nor in *Pride and Prejudice* when it came out in 1813. The author was simply described as being 'a Lady.' Both novels received critical acclaim, and became popular with the reading public. *Mansfield Park* and *Emma* followed in 1814 and 1815 respectively, again anonymously, and enjoyed growing popularity. Jane finished writing *Persuasion* and *Northanger Abbey*, but was beginning to show signs of illness by January 1816 when she started to write a book provisionally entitled *The Brothers*. When it was finally published, over a century later, it bore the title *Sanditon*.

Jane Austen's novels concern themselves more with the gentry and the upper-middle classes than with the aristocracy – and never with the lower strata of society. As the daughter of a rector she would have been on the fringes of the Quality. She was probably more of an observer than a participant, but she understood such essentials as the need for girls to make a good marriage; the need for respectability (and the consequences of its loss); the need to keep up appearances; and the snobbery of 'new money' or 'being trade'.

Jane died on 18 July 1817 and is buried in Winchester Cathedral, having suffered an ailment which has been variously described as Addison's disease, Hodgkin's lymphoma, or a recurrence of the typhus which afflicted her as a child. Others have suggested that she suffered from tuberculosis. Her death at the age of forty-one was followed by the publication of *Persuasion* and *Northanger Abbey* as a set in December 1817. Her brother Henry Austen contributed biographical notes to this posthumous publication, revealing for the first time the true identity of the author.

In her lifetime Jane achieved neither fame nor fortune. Her popularity exploded in the 1880s, and went stratospheric in the century which followed. As a Regency novelist, she combined wit, irony and scathing social commentary. Her novels were romantic stories which reflected the role of women in contemporary society, emphasising the fact that without marriage, a woman could hardly ever be financially independent. Her novels have emerged as a lasting testament to a style of writing which has probably inspired more sequels, prequels and other spin-offs than any other writer.

Left: Jane Austen. (Library of Congress)

Below: The house at Chawton near Alton in Hampshire, where Anne spent the last eight years of her life. (Author's collection)

Jane Austen and Sir Walter Scott were as different as chalk and cheese. Whereas she detested the Prince of Wales and all that he represented (and was only cajoled into dedicating *Emma* to him because she felt that she had no choice, having been asked to do so after a visit to Carlton House), Scott and the prince got on extremely well. By the time the prince had been made regent, Scott was already a famous and highly successful author, playwright and poet, with a huge following both in Britain and in North America. He had endeared himself to the prince by leading a campaign to locate the 'Honours of Scotland' – the Crown Jewels of Scotland last seen at the coronation of Charles II, and hidden away ever since. Scott led a search party down into the depths of Edinburgh Castle, located the Honours, and as a reward was given a baronetcy. When it came to stage-managing the visit to Scotland of the newly crowned King George IV in 1820, Scott was asked to make all the arrangements. In less than one month he arranged the entire royal schedule, with balls, banquets and civic receptions, but

Sir Walter Scott. (Library of Congress, LOT 13407, no. 182)

more importantly he instilled a sense of pride and belonging to the Scots who had for so long been looked down upon as thieves and vagabonds. Scott helped introduce the idea of the kilt – even for the lowland Scots who had never worn them, and of the clan tartan. In doing so he helped create a national identity, and encouraged the new king's love of pageantry and colourful traditions.

By profession Scott was a prominent lawyer. Feeling that some of his historical novels might undermine his authority as a judge and Clerk of Session, he had published *Waverley* anonymously. Later novels, although not part of a series, were termed 'the *Waverley* Novels' because Scott had agreed that they could be inscribed with the words 'by the author of *Waverley*.' Later works were published in his own name. They generally deal with times of conflict – between the Scots and the English (*Rob Roy*) between the Saxons and the Norman French (*Ivanhoe*) and between Christians and Muslims (*The Talisman*). He helped popularise the historical novel as a new genre, with works marked by the sympathetic insights given to the lives of the central characters, whether they were rich and powerful, or poor and dispossessed. Scott wrote of a world of chivalry, of romance and gallantry. He died in 1832, just two years after the death of George IV.

6

PAINTING AND SCULPTURE

When the Royal Academy opened its doors to students in 1768, presided over by the towering figure of Sir Joshua Reynolds, it took a generation to make its mark with new talent. Before then, there was no obviously 'British School of Art', and painting styles were dominated by continental influences. However, once the alumni of the Royal Academy really hit their stride in the Regency period the art world was transformed. Four painters stand out, each in their own very different way: Thomas Lawrence, J. M. W. Turner, John Constable and William Blake. They helped define the Romantic movement, producing paintings which captured the emotions, from love to fear, from hatred to wonderment.

The Regent himself was something of a magpie collector – he acquired paintings obsessively, whether they were by Rembrandt, Rubens or Van Dyke, or by English artists such as Lawrence, Stubbs or Gainsborough. He also invested heavily in fine porcelain, acquiring one of the largest collections of Sèvres in the world, including the dinner service made for Louis XVI. In addition he bought sculptures, by artists such as Canova, Chantrey and Nollekens. He also helped encourage the move to open a National Gallery, open to the public, to display the country's finest paintings. Parliament finally gave the go-ahead to acquire premises in Trafalgar Square a year after George IV had died, but the nucleus of the collection had been bought by the nation some seven years earlier from the banker John Julius Angerstein. Encouraged by the Prince Regent, painting became highly fashionable and attendance at the Royal Academy's Summer Exhibition became a popular part of the social calendar. By 1821 well over 1,100 paintings and sculptures were on display in the Summer Exhibition.

THOMAS LAWRENCE

Born in Bristol in 1769 this child prodigy went on to become the leading portrait painter of the Regency; anybody who was anybody had their portrait painted by

Papier mache snuffbox with a portrait of the Regent, after Sir Thomas Lawrence. (Yale Center for British Art)

him. Until he was eighteen he was entirely self-taught. From the age of ten he had been earning a living supporting his parents by sketching portraits in pastels. His father was a bankrupt innkeeper and young Thomas would earn a few guineas painting commissions from the wealthy tourists attending Bath in order to take the waters. He moved up to London and was introduced to Reynolds, who urged him to study landscape painting. Portraiture was his love, and astonishingly he received a commission to paint a portrait of Queen Charlotte when he was a mere twenty-one years old. Always a charmer with young ladies, Lawrence was something of a hit with the royal princesses when he called to paint their mother's portrait. She, however, found him presumptuous and refused to pay for the painting, which shows her as a 'snow queen' shut away in her palace, and the painting remained in his studio until his death in 1830. He was elected as an Associate of the Royal Academy in 1791 and became a full member three years later. When Sir Joshua Reynolds died, Lawrence succeeded him as Painter in Ordinary to the king. He went on to be knighted, and to become President of the Royal Academy. He held the position throughout the ten years prior to his death, and was undoubtedly the most influential portrait painter of the period. He was inextricably linked with the Romantic movement, with paintings full of emotion and light, but combined with technical accuracy. He was a superlative draughtsman, who spent almost all the money he ever made on collecting drawings by the Old Masters. As a result he never had any money, being described

Portrait of Sir John Moore, by Sir Thomas Lawrence. (© National Portrait Gallery, London)

later as being 'always in love, always in debt'. He was practically penniless when he died, although the sale of his collection of Old Masters was just sufficient to pay off his numerous creditors.

One of the reasons for his impecunious existence, set against his continual popularity, was that he was no good at business. He accepted commissions and then took years and years to complete them. Twelve years to finish a portrait was not unheard of. At his death many paintings were still lined up in his studio waiting for the finishing touches to be applied. And then there was his love life: it would appear from his female portraiture, at which he was especially skilled, that he had great difficulty in avoiding the charms of his sitters. He was a man who fell in love easily. He also had an unfortunate attraction to the daughters of the great Georgian actress Sarah Siddons. He fell in love with the elder daughter Sally, but after a while ditched her for her sister Mary, before deciding to return his attentions to Sally. Mary became ill and died, but not before extracting a promise from her sister that she would never marry Lawrence. Sally went even further – she never spoke to her suitor ever again. Then she too fell ill and died, and Lawrence suffered a complete breakdown. Remarkably, he stayed on reasonable terms with their mother and went on to paint several portraits of her.

His friendship with the Prince of Wales led to him being given the prestigious job of painting the leading figures of the war with France (see earlier) and this entailed visits to the continent where he painted the Pope, the Emperor and the Archduke of Austria, the Russian Tsar, and other leaders. When he died, just five months before the king, he was buried in St Paul's Cathedral, and one of the mourners was J. M. W. Turner, who subsequently sketched the funeral scene.

JOSEPH MALLORD WILLIAM TURNER

Turner was another of the English Romantic painters with a humble background. He was born in 1775 to a mother who was a butcher's daughter. She was admitted to a mental hospital when he was ten years old. His father was an impoverished peruke maker and barber, and even before his teens his son was drawing scenes which were exhibited for sale in his father's shop. At the age of fourteen he enrolled as a student at the Royal Academy, displaying an aptitude for architectural and topographical subjects.

In 1802 he joined the throng of people heading for France to take advantage of the lull in hostilities, studying at the Louvre before heading for Switzerland. When he returned he had already mastered the technique which made him famous – 'capturing light', and recording the ferocity of nature in storms at sea,

J. M. W. Turner's *Venice, from the Porch of Madonna della Salute*. Bequest of Cornelius Vanderbilt. (Metropolitan Museum of Art. Accession Number: 99.31)

bewitching sunrises, violent thunderstorms and the destructive power of fires. 'Moody' and 'ethereal' were characteristic qualities of his paintings, which often featured stunning sunsets, especially after 1816 – the year without a summer. The year saw not just the worst famine of the century in Europe, but also spectacular sunsets caused by volcanic ash high in the earth's atmosphere. Over time, Turner's works became forerunners of the Impressionist movement. He became a wealthy man before dying in 1851 and was buried next to Sir Joshua Reynolds in St Paul's Cathedral. He had never married and bequeathed his collection of paintings to the nation on condition that they were displayed in one place (a condition which has never been fulfilled). His legacy, apart from the purely numerical one of over 500 oil paintings and 2,000 water colours, has been immense.

JOHN CONSTABLE

Born a year after Turner, and into an atmosphere of middle-class gentility, John Constable went on to be loathed by Turner. The latter despised him for his

Salisbury Cathedral from the Bishop's Grounds by John Constable. (Bequest of Mary Stillman Harkness, Metropolitan Museum of Art. Accession Number: 50.145.8)

William Blake's seventh plate from a series entitled *The First Book of Urizen*. (Yale Center for British Art)

well-to-do middle-class background, his education, and for what he saw as his airs and graces, and objected to Constable being admitted to the Royal Academy. As a result, Constable was not elected as a member until he was fifty-two. Nowadays he is recognised as a towering figure in British art, but it has to be remembered that he did not sell a single large canvas in Britain in his lifetime, and what success he enjoyed was largely in France and not in Britain. He eked a precarious living as an artist, being compelled to paint portraits rather than his beloved Suffolk landscapes. Eventually he was invited to lecture at the Royal Academy, but only towards the end of his life, and by then it was too late for him to reap the rewards of becoming an establishment figure. He referred to the Royal Academy as 'the cradle of British Art', maintaining that no great painter was ever entirely self-taught.

He loved painting in the part of the Suffolk border now known as 'Constable country' – the area around his family home at East Bergholt by the River Stour. His best known works include 'Dedham Vale', 'The Hay Wain' and various scenes of Salisbury Cathedral, all of them painted in the Regency period. Unlike Lawrence and Turner, he was happily married, and was distraught when his wife Maria died in 1828, leaving him to bring up seven children. Despite his success in France, where his followers included artists who went on to found the Barbizon school, he declined to travel abroad, saying in a letter to a friend 'I would rather be a poor man [in England] than a rich man abroad.' He died in 1837 and is buried in the family tomb in High Hampstead, London, next to his wife and two of his children.

WILLIAM BLAKE

If Constable was the conformist, Blake was the exact opposite. He attended the Royal Academy between 1779 and 1785, developing a loathing for Reynolds that amounted to outright contempt. In 1808 he published his vitriolic *Annotations to Sir Joshua Reynolds' Discourses* in which he attacked many of the guiding principles which Reynolds had propounded. Blake generally disliked oil painting, criticised the works of Titian, Rembrandt and Rubens, and went on to develop his own highly individualistic style. In his lifetime he was frequently dismissed as a deranged madman, possibly on account of his paranoia and excessive religious mania. He saw angels in the trees, he held conversations with his dead brother, he had an obsession with the wrath of God, and he was obsessed with the very real terrors of Hell, rather than with the delights of Heaven. His paintings were dominated by religious thoughts, and he often illustrated passages from the Old Testament. He also came out with some thought-provoking quotes, including:

'Think in the morning. Act in the noon. Eat in the evening. Sleep in the night.'
'To see the world in a grain of sand, and to see heaven in a wild flower, hold infinity in the palm of your hand, and eternity in an hour.'
'It is easier to forgive an enemy than to forgive a friend.'

Blake's works may never have been appreciated in his lifetime, but they were an inspiration to many subsequent artists. His poetry ('Tyger! Tyger! burning bright, In the forests of the night...') and his contribution to printmaking have been enormously influential. In the words of William Wordsworth: 'There was no doubt that this poor man was mad, but there is something in the madness of this man which interests me more than the sanity of Lord Byron and Walter Scott.' Blake was fiercely opposed to the established church, and when he died in 1827 at the age of sixty-nine he was buried in the dissenters' graveyard at Bunhill Fields. He left behind a wife, the long-suffering Catherine, to whom he had been married for nearly forty-five years.

In sculpture, classical styles dominated the Regency period, especially following the arrival of the Elgin Marbles and discoveries at Pompeii by brothers

The Three Graces by William Wyon, 1817. (Gift in memory of Ignazio Peluso, Metropolitan Museum of Art. Accession Number: 2002.205.3)

Pietro and Ferdinand la Vega in the period up to 1810. John Flaxman had initially established his reputation as a modeller for Josiah Wedgwood but went on to produce funerary sculptures and relief sculptures of great quality. He was appointed Professor of Sculpture at the Royal Academy in 1810. One of his pupils was William Wyon, a brilliant medallist and engraver of the neo-classical school who was appointed chief engraver at the Royal Mint and designed many of the most memorable coins of the late Regency and early Victorian period. Sir Francis Legatt Chantrey was perhaps the most prominent portrait sculptor of his age, and most unusually, was largely self-taught and independent of continental influences. A more controversial figure was Anne Seymour Damer. The god-daughter of Horace Walpole, she made sculptures in bronze, marble and terracotta working from her studio at Walpole's Twickenham home at Strawberry Hill. Being a female sculptor attracted considerable opposition and she was also ridiculed for her manly style of dressing and her close personal friendships with author Mary Berry and the **actress Elizabeth Farren.**

7

HOMES AND FURNISHINGS

In architecture, the Regency period saw two distinctive styles being developed. It was in effect a staging post between the Palladian-inspired buildings, heavily influenced by Roman and renaissance styles, popular a century earlier, and the Gothic Revival styles so favoured by the Victorians. No doubt encouraged to take risks by the patronage of wealthy clients such as the Prince of Wales, architects such as Henry Holland and James Wyatt developed the neo-classical style, often using new materials. Not all of these stood the test of time, but in particular the use of stucco (moulded plaster) in place of stone greatly reduced traditional building costs. Many of the terraces were actually rather badly built, with rubble infill between dividing walls, or strengthened with iron bars which subsequently deteriorated. The builders were not even aiming for building longevity, since most houses were sold on leases of between sixty and ninety-nine years. It was assumed that the building, and particularly the stucco frontage, would need to be completely refurbished, or even rebuilt, at the end of the lease.

The Regency period is perhaps most famous for its terraces of houses – as in Regent Street and Regent's Park in London, along with parts of Pimlico and Mayfair. Brighton (especially Kemp Town) and Tunbridge Wells have other examples. Cheltenham, which prides itself as being the country's most complete Regency town, has particularly fine period housing in Montpellier and in the shopping area of the Promenade, while its borough council is housed in a suitably impressive setting. Royal Leamington Spa, especially in the Parade and Lansdowne Crescent, is noteworthy. In Bristol, Royal York Crescent had been started in the early 1790s but work had virtually stopped during the building recession which marked the last decade of the century. The work started up again, and the development was finished during the Regency period.

Everywhere, the terraced house was seen as a way of accommodating the demand for housing the maximum number of people onto greenfield sites. Particularly influential was the architect Sir John Soane, who built up a large

Bristol's Royal York Crescent, with its wrought-iron railings and delicate balconies. (Author's collection)

Cheltenham's Regency Council Offices. (Author's collection)

collection of drawings of buildings and included them in a series of lectures given to the Royal Academy in his capacity as Professor of Architecture. On the day before and after his lectures he would open his house at Lincoln's Inn Fields so that students could examine his collection of drawings, books, models and antiquities. It became known as an 'Academy of Architecture' and when Soane died in 1837 the house passed to trustees to be maintained as a museum. Many of Soane's drawings relate to the different rates or classes of terraced house, from the first rate occupying 900 square feet, on to the second rate at 500 square feet and down to the fourth rate at less than 350 square feet. The wealthy might live in a building in a terrace with a double frontage, occupying six or seven storeys. Fourth-rate premises would be single frontage and might only extend to three storeys plus a basement.

The top floor was usually set aside for the servants' quarters, with low ceilings, and perhaps a garret window. The floor below would be for bedrooms and nursery for the children, and below that the main bedrooms. The floor below that would be given over to reception and drawing rooms, reached by the staircase leading up from the main entrance hall. On this, the floor level with the front door, would be situated the dining room and morning room, and the library. The floor underneath would constitute the kitchen area with larders, pantries and so on, and below that would be a cellar used for storage of dry goods and coal.

Individual houses in such a terrace typically had a flight of stone steps leading up from the pavement to a wooden front door, invariably painted black, with reeded pilasters or columns at either side. In the early years of the century, iron rather than brass was the norm for the door knocker and doorknob. Usually there would be a semi-circular glass panel known as the fanlight above the door, allowing light into the hall, which was typically tiled with black and white tiles laid in a geometric pattern. The fanlight often featured standard shapes such as circles, loops and spider webs, usually mass-produced offsite to designs chosen from pattern books. Bow-fronted windows were popular, often with very fine glazing bars. Sash windows at first floor level might give access on to a balcony lined with intricate and sometimes feathery metalwork screens.

Fashionable houses of the period would have elaborate plaster cornices around the edge of the ceiling, and, as the ceilings became lower the higher up the house you went, the cornices became smaller and less elaborate. Broad skirting boards were complemented by dado rails fixed roughly thirty-six inches above floor level to prevent chair-backs from damaging the wallpaper which, traditionally in the Regency era, was decorated with vertical stripes and often used water-silk finishes. The Regency saw a plethora of new paint finishes become popular – with rag rolling, stencilling and dragging being used often in imitation of more expensive finishes such as marble. Below the dado rail the skirting boards might be left unpainted and plain, but the door-cases were often elaborately ornamented with scrolls, fruit and festoons of flowers. The doors themselves were usually painted if made out of cheaper woods such as pine, but left in their natural state if made of the more expensive mahogany. In the previous century the actual doors had usually contained six panels. The Regency brought the simpler four-panel door into vogue. Fireplaces were often made of marble in the Adam style, but occasionally would exhibit a somewhat exuberant frieze across the top of carved figures at play, supported by jambs at either side representing classical figures. Inside the hearth a simple steel and brass dog-grate would suffice. The upper rooms of the house would see simpler fireplaces and ever smaller grates.

Regency fireplace. (Museum of Philadelphia)

Above left: Regency chandelier. (The Elisha Whittelsey Collection, Metropolitan Museum of Art. Accession Number: 62.659.54)

Above right: Regency chandelier. (Friends of the American Wing Fund, Metropolitan Museum of Art. Accession Number: 68.177.1)

The Regency period saw a more accurate interpretation of ancient, classical styles. Instead of just following Roman styles, popularised in previous centuries by Inigo Jones, new designs incorporating columns and architectural details borrowed from Ancient Greece became popular. Fluted Ionic columns made a grand reappearance along with Greek key motifs applied to every surface. At Northington, in Hampshire, a neo-classical version of an ancient Greek temple was commissioned in 1804, with a giant Doric portico. It made the Grange one of the earliest Greek Revival-style houses in Europe. Belsay Hall in Northumberland was started in 1807 and finished ten years later. It is a country house built in the Greek style, with rooms constructed around a central courtyard lined with columns. These Doric columns were inspired by designer Sir Charles Monck Middleton's honeymoon visit to Athens. By the time the house was finished, the final consignment of the Elgin Marbles had arrived in Britain in 1812. These decorative friezes had been removed from the Parthenon in Athens and were purchased from Lord Elgin by the British government in 1816, and placed on display in the British Museum where they helped fuel a public fascination with classical designs. Decorative features containing egg-and dart-mouldings appeared, while the Greek anthemion design was adapted as the palmette, with its symmetrical 'fronds' resembling a palm leaf. Along with the Greek key motif it appeared in friezes, on furniture, and soft furnishings and on glassware. Lyre-backed chairs came into vogue along with decorations such as candelabra mounted on Jasperware bases, made in Wedgwood's factory and featuring classical Greek scenes.

Thomas Hope, the first person to coin the phrase 'interior decoration', had written an influential book entitled *Household Furniture and Decoration* in which he set out the importance of matching the style of the architecture to the interior furnishings and decorations. The book was published in 1807 and reflected the work he had commissioned at his home in Duchess Street, off Portland Place, which he had bought from Robert Adam in 1799. His designs were quickly picked up in trade journals and design catalogues, while selected guests could also see his designs for themselves by visiting him at home either at Duchess Street or at his country retreat at Deepdene in Surrey. Above all Hope promoted classical harmony and purity – design elements should flow through from the architecture to the furniture, decorations, fabrics and effects. Hope was a great collector and designer and when he opened his house to the public in 1802 he did so with a grand party attended by the Prince of Wales. Some of his designs were highly innovative and unusual. He had an Egyptian Room, a number of Vase Rooms, and a room given over to Greek and Roman statuary.

Bristol Blue wine-glass coolers decorated with palmette design (left) and a decanter stand with Greek Key design (right). (Courtesy of Bristol Blue Glass (South West) Ltd)

The Regency period was also marked by the appearance of designs influenced by Ancient Egypt. When Napoleon undertook his Egyptian campaign a number of French archaeologists started to explore the ancient temples and to send back artefacts. J-D Vivant-Denon, appointed by Napoleon as Director of Museums from 1802 to 1815, was hugely influential in creating the craze for all things Egyptian. He accompanied Napoleon to Egypt, faithfully recording the key elements of design and decoration. His drawings were published in 1802 and quickly crossed the Channel to herald a period of Egyptian-inspired decorations epitomised in the Egyptian Dining Room at Goodwood House, and by the Egyptian Room in Hope's Duchess Street home mentioned earlier.

The vogue for Egyptian styling was accompanied by sofas set on crocodile legs, or ornamented with the carved head of Isis. Winged sun-discs appeared in even the darkest Regency corner, and tables which would have been familiar to Rameses II made a revival after 3,000 years. Sphinxes were made into pedestals, and foot-stools supported on lion's legs made an appearance. Oddly, although the obelisk now termed Cleopatra's Needle was gifted to Britain in 1819 it was not actually erected in this country for a further sixty years. The obelisk had been given by the Egyptian ruler in commemoration of the naval victories of Lord Nelson at the Battle of the Nile, and of Sir Ralph Abercromby at the Battle of Alexandria, both in 1801. Although the obelisk languished in Alexandria until 1877, the fashion for Egyptiana extended to sculpture and statuary. Copy-cat designs were applied to both the inside and outside of fashionable homes across the country.

These architectural styles, harking back to ancient times, developed at the same time as a return to the medieval gothic design. Horace Walpole with his 'Strawberry Hill Gothic' half a century earlier had shown what could be done by adapting Gothic architectural features. Purists such as Augustus Pugin (father of the more famous Augustus Welby Pugin) insisted on a more accurate interpretation of medieval designs, and the father-and-son collaboration led to publication of the *Specimens of Gothic Architecture* (published between 1821 and 1823) and to *Examples of Gothic Architecture* (1828–31). Both books appeared towards the end of the Regency period and were to be highly influential on subsequent generations of architects.

Overall, the style of early nineteenth-century buildings reflected everything which made things feel 'Regency' – a sense of effortless and refined elegance. In contrast, perhaps the most famous 'Regency' building is the Royal Pavilion at Brighton, since it encapsulates just about all the contemporary trends, and more besides. Technically it is in the Indo-Saracenic style with Chinoiserie interiors, which is another way of saying that it was an extraordinary mish-mash of conflicting and overlapping styles, Indian outside and Chinese inside. As such it reflected the enthusiasm of the Regent to break the rules and try out anything new – especially if it was bright, colourful and exotic. It also reflects his vision of himself as a great emperor, matching anything which China had to offer. It really is a most extraordinary building and the Chinoiserie interiors and furnishings were no less startling than the exterior. Regency furniture broadly corresponds with Biedermeier in Germany and with French Empire in France, but at Brighton there was just that extra bit of gilding, that extra bit of bling.

In general Regency furniture was fine, elegant and balanced. The designs of Sheraton typified the age, and were used on elegant Pembroke (drop-leaf) tables, and on serpentine sideboards and side cabinets. Exotic woods such as burl yew, satinwood, ebonised flame mahogany and flame walnut were much in evidence,

'The court at Brighton à la Chinese!!' by George Cruikshank, 1816, showing the corpulent George IV as a Chinese emperor attended by courtiers. On the king's right sits Lady Hertford, mistress to the king until 1819, and on his left his daughter, who is suggesting that she should be married off 'to a Chinaman instead of getting me a husband among our German cousins'. (Lewis Walpole Library)

along with mother-of-pearl inlays and elaborate marquetry. The rarer tulipwood and zebrawood were expensive but fashionable and were used mostly in veneers, inlays and lattice or string work. Where cheaper soft-woods such as pine, elm or beech were used they would often be painted light green and dusted with metallic powder to give the effect of patinated bronze. Marble tops on wooden pedestals were fashionable. Brass and gilt handles were much in evidence, and sabre legs (curved like the blade of a sabre) supported chairs, tables and sideboards. Curtains often matched the fabric used in chair backs and sofas and were typically made of rich chintz or heavy damask brocades. Above all, the low-backed sofa with wooden scroll ends, inlaid brass decoration, and with tasselled bolsters at each end and covered with elegant damask fabric, came to typify the age.

Regency sofa. (Metropolitan Museum of Modern Art. Gift of C. Ruxton Love Jr. Accession Number: 60.4.1)

8

THE INDUSTRIAL REVOLUTION

Many of the inventions which are associated with the early phases of the Industrial Revolution started to bear fruit in the Regency period. For instance, James Watt, in partnership with Matthew Boulton, had already developed a method of using his steam-powered machines to produce rotational power for weaving, grinding and milling. Their steam engines were already being manufactured in their hundreds for use in mines, but their influence on society did not stop when the Watt–Boulton partnership came to an end in 1800. Watt and Boulton passed their shares in the business to their respective sons and, under their control, the business continued to expand. Watt carried on inventing – often not bothering to patent his ideas. Boulton devoted his energies to perfecting ways of improving the currency, and it was his machinery which was installed in the Royal Mint when it moved out of the Tower of London to new premises a few hundred yards away. In 1816 the Great Re-coinage took place. A period of high inflation and high taxation (linked to the cost of the war with France) had led to the need for new coins to help back up the largely unpopular paper currency developed in the 1790s. Out went the twenty-one shilling guinea and in came the twenty-shilling sovereign. More importantly, vast quantities of silver coins were minted, with some 40 million one shilling coins being minted in the four years up to 1820, along with millions of crowns, half-crowns and lower denominations. Out went the cumbersome and heavy 'cartwheel' pennies, and in came much smaller pennies, halfpennies and farthings.

The re-coinage became one of the most visible examples of the change brought to everyday living as the Industrial Revolution gathered pace. The power of the steam engine helped factories develop – manufacturers were no longer dependent on running water or horses to provide power. Whole industries were transformed, starting with the textile industry. Manchester was nicknamed 'Cottonopolis' because of the plethora of textile factories which developed in the early 1800s. Older cottage industries, where home-workers were paid on a piece-rate basis for

A View of Murton Colliery near Seaham, County Durham by J. W. Carmichael. (Yale Center for British Art. Paul Mellon Collection B1976.7.12)

COINAGE DENOMINATIONS AFTER THE GREAT RE-COINAGE

Gold
Sovereign (one pound) – equivalent to twenty shillings
Half-sovereign – equivalent to ten shillings
Silver
Crown – equivalent to five shillings
Half-crown – equivalent to two shillings and sixpence
Shilling – equivalent to twelve pennies
Sixpence
Groat – equivalent to four pence
Threepence
Copper
Penny – equivalent to 1/240th of a pound
Halfpenny
Farthing – equivalent to one quarter of a penny

items which they produced, gave way to fully mechanised factories churning out vast quantities of cheap goods. The drift into cities was well-marked by the start of the Regency period, with sprawling new towns struggling to cope with the influx of rural migrants. Towns and cities simply did not have the infrastructure to cope with the demands placed on them – in particular for hygienic supplies of water and drainage and sewerage, as well as for roads and adequate housing. It was ironic that a revolution which was to increase national incomes and productivity first started by creating poverty and poorer living conditions.

WILLIAM MURDOCH

As an engineer working for Boulton and Watt, Murdoch had spent his early career in Cornwall working out problems associated with the use of steam engines in deep mines. It was when he moved to Birmingham, eventually becoming a partner in the firm, that his full range of talents appeared. He is credited as having invented the oscillating cylinder steam engine, along with the steam gun, the pneumatic tube messaging system, and various innovations linked to the steam engine such as the 'D slide valve' and the 'sun and planet gear'. He was at the forefront of the development of gas lighting, and is credited with having lit his home in Redruth, Cornwall by gas in the 1790s. He went on to become a hugely influential marine engineer. He was also a chemist who developed a new form of isinglass (used in the brewing industry to remove cloudiness from beer). He died in 1839, his contribution to the Industrial Revolution largely overshadowed by James Watt and Matthew Boulton. All three are commemorated in the statue known as The Golden Boys, a gilded bronze memorial to three giants of the Industrial Revolution, erected in Birmingham.

GAS LIGHTING

Few of the changes brought into the public eye during the Regency were as dramatic as the introduction of gas lighting. Under Murdoch's influence, gas lighting was installed outside the Boulton and Watt factory premises at Soho in Birmingham in 1802 to celebrate the Peace of Amiens. It caused a sensation. Within five years whole factories were being illuminated in this way, and, suddenly, lighting was reliable and efficient. This led to the introduction of new work patterns such as shift systems. By 1807 Frederic Albert Winsor was demonstrating that gas could be piped under the pavement from his home in Pall Mall, to feed thirteen lamps erected in the street outside and stretching from St James's to Cockspur Street. By 1813 Winsor's Gas Light and Coke Company had acquired a royal charter to run gas pipes throughout the City of London, Westminster and Southwark. The company enjoyed a monopoly in those areas for twenty-one years, and almost immediately gas companies in other cities followed suit, so that by 1820 many cities throughout the country were using this form of illumination.

The rapid spread of lighting led to a huge demand for coal and to the development of coking plants. By-products included ammonia and carbolic acid, and coal tar that was used in used in chemical and dyeing industries. Coke produced during the gas-extraction process was used in place of charcoal and helped reduce the fuel cost for pig iron and wrought iron, and larger blast furnaces became cost-effective. In 1828 the first hot-blast furnace was introduced at a factory in Scotland, whereby air was pre-heated before being injected into the blast furnace. This greatly improved fuel efficiency, allowed for higher temperatures and increased capacity.

Steam power was applied to provide motive power for ships, with James Watt junior and William Murdoch at the forefront of experiments. In 1817 Watt acquired the *Caledonia*, and Murdoch began the task of installing two engines (one for each paddle) and of making the vessel sea-worthy and fuel efficient. Much testing, and victory in races with competitors, resulted in the Boulton and Watt factory receiving orders from both the Royal Navy and commercial ferry operators, and with around fifty vessels being supplied with Boulton and Watt engines in the twelve years up to 1825. Elsewhere, in 1819 the first steam-propelled vessel (the SS *Savannah*) crossed the Atlantic.

The lamp-lighter hurries to work...
(Author's collection)

Interior of an Ironworks by Godfrey Sykes. (Yale Center for British Art, Paul Mellon Collection)

HENRY MAUDSLAY

Henry Maudslay (1771–1831) is regarded as the father of machine tool technology. In 1800 he installed the first screw-cutting lathe, allowing standardisation of screw thread sizes for the first time. Suddenly nuts and bolts were interchangeable and could be manufactured by the thousand, instead of having to be made by hand as individual pairs. He developed lathes capable of producing identical machine parts, and invented a bench-top micrometer screw – which he dubbed 'the Lord Chancellor' – to measure accurately to within one ten thousandth of an inch.

Marc Isambard Brunel (father of Isambard Kingdom Brunel) turned to Maudslay for help in designing the world's first production line, making pulley blocks for the Royal Navy at Portsmouth. It revolutionised an industry to the extent that ten men, in charge of forty-three machines, could produce more blocks than a hundred men could previously have produced by hand – and to a higher, more uniform standard. Maudslay also invented methods for printing calico cloth and for desalinating seawater for ships' boilers.

After 1810 he went into partnership with an admiralty draughtsman called Joshua Field and they specialised in manufacturing steam engines for the Royal Navy. It was this expertise which led, after Maudslay had died, to his company being commissioned to make the giant 750-horsepower engine for Isambard Kingdom Brunel's *Great Western*, the first purpose-built transatlantic steamship.

In 1825 Marc Isambard Brunel had started work on the Thames Tunnel, the first successful attempt to tunnel under a navigable river. Brunel turned to Maudslay to come up with the tunnelling shields needed to protect the workers excavating the tunnel between Rotherhithe and Wapping, and to provide the pumps which kept the river water out. As an engineer he inspired countless others, helping make Britain 'the workshop of the world'.

INDUSTRIALISATION BRINGS PROBLEMS

Working conditions in some of the new factories were poor; men, women and children worked for long hours in often cramped and dangerous conditions and in an era before Health and Safety, accidents were common. In many cases the demand for coal forced mine owners to dig deeper and deeper shafts, with a consequent risk of collapse of mine shafts and of explosions caused by firedamp, where methane and carbon monoxide had built up. In 1812 some ninety-one miners were killed in an explosion at the Felling Mine near Newcastle. This prompted Humphry Davy to develop a safety lamp, but this was not an entire success because it was fragile, easily knocked over or damaged. It did however lead to a greater awareness of the need for safety precautions. At the same time Parliament started to nibble away at the worst of the excesses in factories, passing the Cotton Mills and Factories Act in 1819. It stated that no children under nine were to work in the textile factories. Children from the age of nine to sixteen were restricted to working a maximum of twelve hours a day, and were entitled to breaks, totalling one and a half hours a day, for meals. It was not until 1833 that the Factories Act introduced an effective system of inspectorates, and well into the Victorian era before serious attempts were made to restrict the working day to ten hours, and to provide for healthy work conditions.

TRAVEL AND TRANSPORT

Thomas Telford stands out as one of the foremost civil engineers of the Regency. In the 1790s he had been linked with canal projects such as the Ellesmere Canal and the construction of the spectacular Pontcysyllte Aqueduct at Llangollen (both completed in 1805). He was involved in plans to provide drinking water for Liverpool, the repairs to the old London Bridge and a massive scheme to improve roads in the Scottish Highlands – a project which took over twenty years and involved building nearly a thousand miles of roads, numerous bridges, and the construction of the Caledonian Canal linking the east and west coasts of Scotland. He was commissioned to improve the London to Holyhead highway, necessitating the creation of miles of completely new roads through the inhospitable mountainous area around Snowdonia. He was also responsible for the construction of what was then the world's longest suspension bridge, across the Menai Straits linking Anglesey to the Welsh mainland. In 1820 he was appointed president of the Institution of Civil Engineers, a post he held until his death in 1834. He enjoyed the punning nickname 'Colossus of Roads', a title which could just as easily have been applied to that other great Scottish road engineer, John Loudon McAdam. McAdam had moved to Bristol in 1802 and developed his passion for road building, experimenting with different methods of crushing and laying stones to form a proper road base. Larger stones were broken up by hand, using hammers to produce uniform-sized small stones, which were then bound with a coating of binder as a cementing agent. Later developments involved spraying water on to stone dust to fill the gaps between the larger stones, a process known as water macadamising. Travel became much smoother and more comfortable, although the dust was a problem. It would be another 100 years before tar would be added to the macadam, but in the meantime the macadam road surface made life easier for all road users.

The early nineteenth century saw massive civil engineering projects (linked to establishing a comprehensive canal system throughout the country) reach fruition: canals linked Yorkshire and Lancashire with London, and the burgeoning industries in the West Midlands and the Potteries were linked by a network of narrow canals. But canal-mania was almost immediately overtaken by the advent of the railway, a phenomenon which transformed life in Victorian Britain, but which had its roots firmly in the Regency period. Back in 1804 Trevethick had demonstrated that steam could provide locomotive power for an engine running on rails to pull a heavy load of slate from the quarry at Pen-y-Darren in Wales. By 1825 Stephenson's experiments had led to the opening of the Stockton to Darlington line. His engine 'Locomotion 1' was the first to carry railway passengers, running along a twenty-seven-mile line. In the following year Parliament passed an act permitting the construction of a railway line between Liverpool and Manchester, and in 1829 the Rainhill Trials were held to decide what engines should be used. The line opened in 1830, with the unfortunate MP William Huskisson becoming the first casualty of the Railway. Age, being run over at the official inauguration of the service on 15 September 1830. A mere fifteen years later, thirty million rail passengers a year were being transported by rail, an astonishing explosion of mass transport, transforming the economy and changing the habits of the nation.

View on the Liverpool and Manchester Railway with the Locomotive 'Twin Sisters' in a Siding by Isaac Shaw, *c.* 1830. (Yale Center for British Art, Paul Mellon Collection)

9

KING AT LAST

When George III died on 29 January 1820 his son became king in his own right. This did not bring him any new powers, but it did give him the chance to 'make his own mark'. For some years he had indulged himself that he was the Great Leader, the man who had stood up to Napoleon, the king of a great nation which had come into world dominance under his tutelage. It meant that much of his ten-year reign was given over to conspicuous consumption and extravagance.

First among the problems identified by George IV was his errant wife. She had been behaving badly in her six-year jaunt around Europe, openly parading herself with her presumed lover Pergamo. Worse, when the queen heard that her husband was now king she decided to return to England to resume her role as queen consort. George was desperate to get rid of her but knew that an application through the courts for a divorce would leave him open to cross-examination about his own extramarital affairs and peccadilloes. Accordingly he asked Parliament to pass the Pains and Penalties Bill, which was in effect a trial of Caroline's conduct, carried out in a very public parliamentary arena. The House of Lords was asked to consider the immense amount of evidence pointing to Caroline's adultery. The salacious details were lapped up by an eager public, who tended to side with Caroline rather than with her hypocrite of a husband. The bill was passed by the narrowest of margins, but public opposition to the trial meant that the planned divorce had to be shelved. Public petitions were signed by the thousand: the masses loved Caroline and despised the king in almost equal measure.

The Tory government persuaded the king not to continue with the divorce, and George concentrated his efforts on trying to get her banned from the actual coronation, which was due to be held at Westminster Abbey in July 1821. She, however, announced that she was fully entitled to be present, as queen consort, and turned up at the abbey determined to take her lawful place as queen. The result was an unseemly spat, with the queen and her entourage being turned away

George IV crown, dated 1826.
(Metropolitan Museum of Art.
Gift in memory of Ignazio Peluso.
Accession Number: 2000.224. 6)

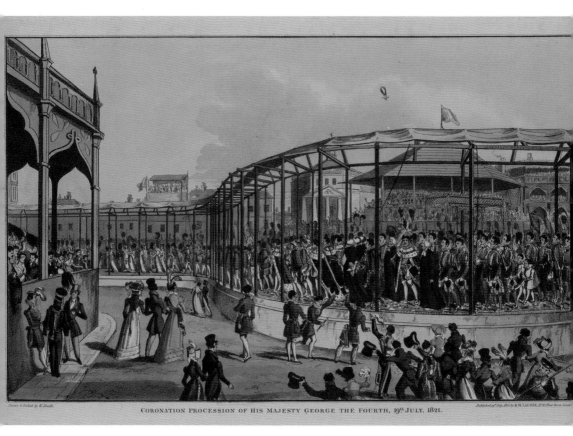

CORONATION PROCESSION OF HIS MAJESTY GEORGE THE FOURTH, 19th JULY. 1821.

The coronation of George IV, depicted by William Heath. (Library of Congress)

'Nero Fiddled When Rome Was Burning', showing George IV playing the cello alongside his mistress Marchioness Elizabeth Conyngham in front of a list of excessive expenses run up by the monarch for his royal palaces. Note the torn-off portrait of the queen (Caroline) on the left. Drawn by William Heath, 1820. (Lewis Walpole Library)

at the point of a bayonet. Public opinion was divided over her conduct, with many people deeming it unregal, but the cartoonists went into overdrive. The day following the coronation the queen fell ill, convinced that she had been poisoned. She may equally have had stomach cancer. She died just three weeks later, leaving question marks over the cause of death. Despite attempts by the government to ban a high-profile demonstration of mourning, her funeral procession travelled through the heart of London to Harwich, where a boat took her remains back to her homeland of Brunswick. She was buried beneath an inscription which reads 'Here lies Caroline, the Injured Queen of England.'

No-one could accuse the new king of stinting on his coronation, a magnificent and sumptuous affair which 'invented' a whole new pageantry to please the king. The astronomical cost (at almost £250,000, roughly twenty-five times the amount of the coronation of George III sixty years earlier) was typical of the new king's reckless disregard for financial control.

In the two years following his accession the king visited Ireland (the first reigning monarch to bother to do so since 1395) and to Scotland, where he enjoyed what was known as 'one and twenty daft days'. The Scottish tour was organised by Sir Walter Scott, and saw the monarch bedecked in a newly envisioned 'tradition' of a tartan kilt, which the king wore comically short, and with a pair of pink tights underneath to disguise his enormously fat legs. The visit was a great success in re-establishing Scottish pride, and in popularising the concept of clan tartans and the kilt as a national dress. The new king also visited Hanover, the first time a Hanoverian monarch had troubled to do so for seventy years. But this push to see every part of his various kingdoms soon wore off and, in his later years, the king became something of a recluse at his home at Windsor Castle. Grossly overweight, in pain from gout, and as a result dependent upon increasingly large doses of laudanum, the king cut a sad figure. It is also likely that he suffered from arteriosclerosis and dropsy (peripheral oedema) and as a result exercised less and less. His waist ballooned to such an extent that by 1824 his corsets were being made with a fifty-inch waist – and he still had six years of overeating to go! Windsor was his prison, and ironically was one of his greatest achievements. He had been involved in three other grand buildings, Carlton House, Buckingham Palace and the Royal Pavilion at Brighton, but with Windsor Castle he influenced all subsequent generations in their perception of what a medieval castle should look like. He used the architect Jeffry Wyatt to remodel much of the old building, creating the skyline we know today. In 1824 Wyatt changed his name to Wyatville, and was knighted for his efforts.

During his regency the prince had constructed the Royal Lodge in Windsor Great Park, but decided to move into the castle when he became king. He felt that the castle was simply not grand enough, and insisted on a complete range of styles, neo-classical, rococo, and gothic. The works cost a staggering £1 million, despite the fact that Parliament had authorised less than a third of that amount. New towers and new state apartments were constructed; the Round Tower was raised in height and a new entrance, the George IV Gateway, was built to give a clear view to the Long Walk in the Great Park. A Grand Corridor was added along two sides of the quadrangle, a new St George's Chapel was built, and

'Windsor Castle from the south' by William Daniell, 1827. (Yale Center for British Art, Paul Mellon Collection)

battlements were added to the tops of all exterior walls. Inside, different rooms were given different treatments – the State Dining Room in high gothic style, the Grand Reception Room in Rococo style, and the White, Green and Crimson Drawing Rooms were filled with items transferred from Carlton House. Gobelin tapestries were acquired, and the foremost furniture makers in the country were employed to fill the rooms with gothic furnishings. A magnificent, larger than life, marble statue of the king was commissioned from Sir Francis Chantrey. George IV moved into the castle in 1828, with some of the work unfinished. When he died, two years later, it was left to his brother (William IV) to finish certain areas such as the Waterloo Chamber, housing portraits of all the Allied leaders.

During his ten-year reign George IV had a diminishing rapport with his ministers. Whereas he was decidedly pro-Whig in his pre-regency days he became increasingly more aligned to the Tories. His prime minister between 1820 and 1827 was Lord Liverpool, a man who the king regularly insulted and intrigued against. Liverpool was succeeded by George Canning and Canning had a slightly easier time of things because he cultivated a friendship with one person the king really trusted – his doctor Sir William Knighton. Knighton had originally been a prominent obstetrician, but had attached himself to the Prince Regent, making himself so invaluable to the somewhat weak-minded monarch that he was given

Royal coat of arms on the gates at Buckingham Palace. (Author's collection)

the task of managing the king's finances and became Keeper of the Privy Purse. He was made auditor of both the duchy of Cornwall and duchy of Lancaster. Royal tradesmen were notified that no goods could be ordered unless this was confirmed in writing by Knighton; slowly the personal finances of the king were put in some sort of order. Knighton retired from his medical practice in 1822 and devoted all his energies to protecting the king's interests, earning much criticism and adverse comment in the process. What is clear is that he served his king well, and in return was trusted implicitly, with the king writing to him as 'my dearest friend,' and signing off 'most affectionately yours' even though convention at the time was for the king to write in the third person.

When Canning died in 1827 after just four months in office, the king increasingly took a back seat, leaving the business of government to the politicians. In time, the Duke of Wellington became Prime Minister and was persuaded that it was politically untenable not to recognise calls for Catholic emancipation. In his pre-regency days, George had appeared to be in favour of allowing Roman Catholics to vote, but as king he apparently felt that it went against his coronation oath, in which he had promised to 'defend the faith' – the faith being the Anglican Church. Wellington eventually persuaded the king to agree to the Catholic Relief Bill but over the next six weeks pressure was brought to persuade the king to revoke his decision, not least by his rabidly anti-Catholic brother the Duke of Cumberland. In March the king changed his mind. The cabinet resigned en masse. The king changed his mind again, and on 13 April

Brighton Pavilion Music Room. (© Royal
Pavilion & Museums, Brighton & Hove)

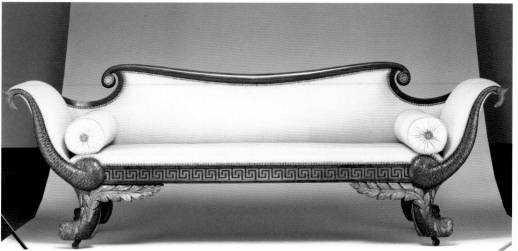

Regency-style sofa, 1820. (Friends of the American Wing Fund, Metropolitan Museum of Art.
Accession Number: 65.58)

1829 the Catholic Relief Act finally received the Royal Assent. It was to prove a spur to the much greater overhaul of the voting arrangements in Britain, with the Great Reform Act (more correctly, the Representation of the People Act) following in 1832.

By 1828 the eyesight of the king was failing, and he was suffering from breathlessness and insomnia. He was a virtual recluse, choosing to hide away from his subjects who regarded him with derision and contempt. His reign degenerated into a sad decline, and he became more and more reclusive. He resorted to increasing quantities of laudanum (and, apparently, cherry brandy). He died on 26 June 1830 and was buried In St George's Chapel at Windsor Castle. The legacy of the Regency period formed the foundation stone for the very different – but highly successful – Victorian era.

A Worcester teacup from 1807–12, made at Worcester porcelain factory. (Philadelphia Museum Accession Number: 1977-96-3nn)

WHAT NEXT?

BOOKS

Austen, Jane, *Sense and Sensibility* (T. Egerton, 1811)

Austen, Jane, *Pride and Prejudice* (T. Egerton, 1813)

Austen, Jane, *Emma* (John Murray, 1815)

Baker, Kenneth, *George IV: A Life in Caricature* (Thames & Hudson, 2005)

English Romantic Poetry: An Anthology (Dover Thrift Editions, 2012)

Forester, C. S., *The Happy Return* (Michael Joseph, 1937)

Forester, C. S., *A Ship of the Line* (Michael Joseph, 1938)

Heyer, Georgette, *Arabella* (William Heinemann, 1949)

Heyer, Georgette, *The Grand Sophy* (William Heinemann, 1950)

Kloester, Jennifer, *Georgette Heyer's Regency World* (William Heinemann, 2005)

Scott, Sir Walter, *Waverley* (A. Constable, 1814)

Scott, Sir Walter, *Rob Roy* (A. Constable, 1817)

Scott, Sir Walter, *Ivanhoe* (A. Constable, 1820)

FILMS AND TV

Beau Brummell: This Charming Man (2006)

Becoming Jane (2007)

Bright Star (2009)

Lady Caroline Lamb (1972)

Pride and Prejudice (1995)

Sharpe (1993–2008)

Vanity Fair (1998)

Vanity Fair (2004)

Waterloo (1970)

BUILDINGS AND PLACES

Brighton Royal Pavilion

Buckingham Palace

Cheltenham town centre

Royal York Crescent, Bristol

Sir John Soane's Museum, 12–14 Lincoln's Inn Fields, London

The Grand Pump Room, Bath

The National Portrait Gallery

The V & A Museum

Windsor Castle

For gardens, see those designed by Humphry Repton, for instance those at Blaise Castle (near Bristol) and Woburn Abbey (Bedfordshire).

INDEX

Also in the Illustrated Introductions series

Fascinated by history? Wish you knew more?
The Illustrated Introductions are here to help.

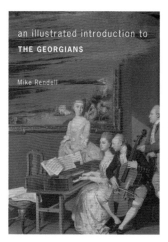

An Illustrated Introduction
to the Georgians

978–1–4456–3630–6

£9.99

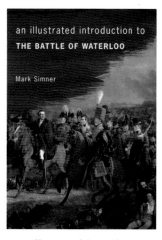

An Illustrated Introduction
to the Battle of Waterloo

978–1–4456–4666–4

£9.99

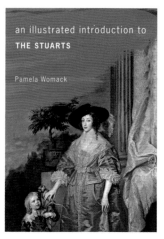

An Illustrated Introduction
to the Stuarts

978–1–4456–3788–4

£9.99

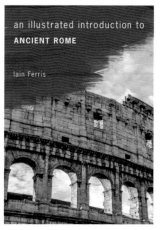

An Illustrated Introduction
to Ancient Rome

978–1–4456–4565–0

£9.99

Available from all good bookshops or to order direct
Please call **01453–847–800**
www.amberley-books.com